MW00898699

To
Bob + Judy
So sorry for the loss
of your son Scott. Trust
that he is still with you.
Best wishes
Barb J Hopkinson
9/26/14

A Butterfly's Journey
Healing Grief After the Loss of a Child

BARBARA J HOPKINSON

Copyright © 2013 by Barbara J Hopkinson.
Edited by Roberta Coffey and Bruce Menin.
Cover Design by Alan Carroll
Swallowtail butterfly design by Newburyport Memorial Art Co

Audio book produced by Roger Ebacher, REBACH Music Studio
Copyright © 2013 by Barbara J Hopkinson
Musical composition, arrangements and performances by Nancy Day,
"Love Everlasting" music and lyrics by Nancy Day and Brent DeLibero,
Copyright © 2013 Nancy Day and Barbara J Hopkinson

Library of Congress Control Number:		2013902748
ISBN:	Hardcover	978-1-4797-9527-7
	Softcover	978-1-4797-9526-0
	Ebook	978-1-4797-9528-4

All rights reserved. No part of this book may be reproduced or transmitted in any form or by any means, electronic or mechanical, including photocopying, recording, or by any information storage and retrieval system, without permission in writing from the copyright owner.

This book is designed to provide information and motivation to our readers. It is sold with the understanding that the author or publisher is not engaged to render any type of psychological, legal, or any other kind of professional advice. The content is the sole expression and opinion of the author, and not necessarily that of the publisher. No warranties or guarantees are expressed or implied by the choice to include any of the content in this volume. Neither the publisher nor the author shall be liable for any physical, psychological, emotional, financial, or commercial damages, including, but not limited to, special, incidental, consequential or other damages. Our views and rights are the same: You are responsible for your own choices, actions, and results.

This book was printed in the United States of America.

Rev. date: 06/07/2013

To order additional copies of this book, contact:
Xlibris Corporation
1-888-795-4274
www.Xlibris.com
Orders@Xlibris.com
73248
or
www.abutterflysjourney.com

Dedication

To my three sons: Brent, Brad, and Robbie.

Table of Contents

Acknowledgements

THERE ARE SO many people to acknowledge and to whom to express gratitude for their help, belief, encouragement, teachings, prayers, and support. My family first: my sons and stepchildren, my current and former husbands and their families, my sister, brother, and their families as well as my Godmother and extended family. Then there are the countless friends, spiritual advisors, and writing mentors, as well as those who helped with the production of my book and related areas. Also very important are all of the bereaved families I've been able to interact with, along with our national support organization, The Compassionate Friends.

I think you know who you are—too many to name individually. I thank you, love you and will always be grateful. This book started with your support before, during, and after the deaths of my children.

Thank you ALL.

Preface

Journey to a New Normal

THE BOOK IS titled *A Butterfly's Journey* because of the symbolism of transition that a butterfly represents and how that symbolism relates to our families. *In his book Butterfly,* Thomas Marent states, *"The life cycle of the butterfly is marked by change; each stage of life— egg, caterpillar, pupa, and adult—is radically different from what comes before."*

I am struck with the similarity to our own lives, and the radical changes we undergo after the loss of a child, grandchild, or sibling. *Marent* also notes that *"in numerous mythologies the butterfly is a symbol of spiritual renewal. The grub-like caterpillar, earthbound and driven by material needs, represents the life of a mortal, while the chrysalis, shrouded and inert, is a metaphor for death. The liberation of the butterfly, miraculously transformed into a being of lightness and grace, symbolizes resurrection"* . . . *and in my mind, afterlife.*

There are thousands of species, shapes, colors, and styles of butterflies as individual as our children. When they emerge from the chrysalis as beautiful winged butterflies, they have short life spans—as do so many of our children. Or we could equate their emergence as a new beginning for them—spreading their wings in their spiritual lives, and we could consider the pupal stage equivalent to our child's life on earth.

Marent also notes that "*in butterfly terms—(life is) as short as a week or as long as a year. Flight brings the butterfly many advantages—liberating it from the confines of its caterpillar world.*" In many cases, our children may be liberated from an illness, depression, or handicaps in taking spiritual flight in their butterfly stage. Like our children, many butterflies live out their lives within a short distance of where they are born, but others embark on journeys of epic proportions, crossing entire continents.

We all go through many transitions in life; I certainly have after losing three children. I believe that families who have lost a child go through even more intense transitions or changes than most other trauma causes. In the natural order of things, our children are not supposed to predecease us. The death of a child rocks our world. Many families come closer together, but some break apart, as my marriage did. We have to adjust to life without our loved one and the impact that has on our families. We also need to adapt to the differences in how each of us grieves.

There is no right or wrong way to grieve although some ways may be healthier than others. I learned much from my own experience and in hearing about the experiences of the grieving families I work with in my support groups—but in particular this: just like a butterfly must go through an ugly stage to reach a beautiful stage, we must go through the grieving process to reach a healthy acceptance stage. You can't avoid it or get around it, or it will be back to haunt you in later years.

Introduction

I WROTE THIS book out of love for my children—all of them, whether I got to really know them or not. My first husband Bob and I were married for thirty years. Our marriage was far from perfect, but it was mostly good. During that time, we lost a baby in a miscarriage then had two wonderful sons, Brent and Brad, that we raised. Our third son, Robbie, was stillborn. Later, Brent died in a motorcycle accident at the age of twenty-one. Brad is thirty now. We had a close, values-based family where both parents actively participated in raising our children, and we were active with our extended families on both sides. Although I now feel blessed that I was able to share my sons' lives, even for a short time, it had been a long journey to achieve the clarity to think of their lives as a gift rather than only a loss, to continue to love each of them in a way that heals us both.

I also wrote this book as part of my grieving and healing process. Through the writing, I am able to share what I have learned. The experience of each loss is deeply and ultimately personal; it has its own context and its own unique impact. It is important to recognize that we all grieve differently, even within the same family. Our losses are not more or less significant, and it may not be constructive to compare them to one another. As I move through my own journey and connect with others who have lost children, I found that there are common elements of grief that I shared with those parents, siblings, grandparents, family, and friends.

Of greatest importance, I write this book primarily to share my experience and evolution in response to the deaths of my children at three very different stages. Each of these losses shook me to the core, bringing about significant changes in my life, in my beliefs, in my relationships, and in how I experienced the world. My hope is that this book will help other bereaved families get through their ordeals. I've lost parents, grandparents, and many other family members and friends, but the loss of a child is like nothing else I've experienced. It is the hardest thing that I've had to endure. I would not wish it on anyone, not even an enemy. But if you are part of this *"club that no one wants to belong to,"* I hope this book helps you in some way.

My focus in telling this story is on Brent, my twenty-one-year-old son, but this is not his biography. I'd also like to describe briefly the impact of my first trimester miscarriage during my first pregnancy when I didn't know what to expect, but was so hopeful. In addition, I will relate what it was like to go through a near-full-term stillbirth with my third son Robbie when I was familiar with giving birth, raising children, and fully expected everything to be normal as it had been with my two older boys.

My family is certainly different now than I imagined it

would be at this stage in my life. My surviving son, Brad, is the most important thing in my life. He endured the loss of his older and younger brothers. We became even closer and more protective of each other. We learned together. It made us both more intuitive, more in touch with ourselves and enabled a better understanding of each other.

This book began as an unexpected act of grace by Brad. Six months after Brent's death and facing our first Christmas without him, Brad, then nineteen, went into a bookstore—not a common occurrence for him then. He emerged with my Christmas gift—a beautiful, refillable, leather-bound journal; this despite the fact that neither of us had ever kept a diary before. He paid for it with his own money, not easy for him at the time.

His choice was perfect, and out of that journal, this book was born. I understood immediately that I should try writing down my feelings and was amazed at how cathartic it was. Years later, I'm on my ninth refill for that now-beaten-up leather journal. The journaling helped me work through my grief and the loss of my thirty-year marriage after Brent's death, when I was still raw emotionally.

This story is told from a mother's viewpoint since I can only write it from my own memory, journals, insights, and feelings. Still, it describes experiences and circumstances of a family and their community, and so I've brought in the perspective which other family members shared with me.

It feels to me that genders grieve very differently. From what I observed between my husband, son, and myself and also from observing the parents I work with, in the support chapter that I founded one year after Brent's death. This still exists as a local chapter of the Compassionate

Friends, an international organization whose mission is to support bereaved families after the loss of a child at any age (www.compassionatefriends.org).

Our backgrounds and personalities influence our style of grief too, of course. There are no rules; we are all unique and should follow our instincts about what works for us, learning and adjusting as we go. I believe in trusting your own gut rather than other people's opinions. We all have some level of intuition we can listen to. There is value to the wisdom we acquire in the moment as well as the wisdom born of hindsight and reflection. If nothing else, I've gained some hard-earned wisdom from these experiences that helped me move forward, even though I acknowledge that given a choice, this is not the method I would have chosen to become wiser.

We are "recovering bereaved parents," and like recovering alcoholics, we find that the loss of a child is something you never completely "get over". But the grief becomes less "in your face" over time. That loss is with you always, but you learn to find a "new normal." Hopefully, you will find joy again and come to understand that your child's life was a gift to you, not just a loss. That's what I have come to understand. It is what your children would want—that you focus more on the love then the grief. It is more healing for everyone.

I firmly believe that my sons' spirits continue and that I still have a relationship with them, just in a different way. I believe that is true of all of our children that have passed on, no matter what the circumstances.

Elizabeth Kubler-Ross is the writer whose research into grief introduced the world to the now famous "five stages of grief," a series of emotional responses to the experience of loss that most people work their way through as they become reconciled to their life after loss. These stages, noted below, provide a good framework for understanding their journey, and I will be referring to them throughout part 1 of the book. Others have since augmented EKR's work as well.

The Swiss psychiatrist Elizabeth Kübler-Ross spent years with the terminally ill and dying, and in the process, she learned a great deal about how individuals handle death. In 1969, she published her findings in the famous book, "On Death and Dying." In it, she theorized that people pass through five distinct stages when they are grieving and that these stages can come in any order and are distinctive to the individual.

"Each of us moves through these stages in our own way. They can occur in sequence, but often occur in ways that feel random or repetitive. We might think we are finished with a stage only to wake up and find ourselves bargaining, or angry, or even in denial again. They simply offer a tool for reflection; and hopefully they will help you to treat yourself more gently and with greater compassion on this journey - each in your own way, each in your own time."
Elisabeth Kübler-Ross and David Kessler

DENIAL
This first stage of grieving helps us to survive the loss. The world becomes meaningless and overwhelming. Life makes no sense. We are in a state of shock and denial . . . It is nature's way of letting in only as much as we can handle.

ANGER
Anger is necessary for healing. Be willing to feel your anger even though it may seem endless. The truth is that anger has no limits. It can extend not only to your friends, the doctors, your family, yourself, and your loved one who died but also to God.

BARGAINING
It seems like you will do anything if only your loved one would be spared. The "if onlys" cause us to find fault in ourselves and what we "think" we could have done differently. We will do anything not to feel the pain of this loss. We try to negotiate our way out of the hurt.

DEPRESSION
Grief enters our lives on a deeper level. This depressive stage feels as though it will last forever. It's not a sign of mental illness, but an appropriate response to a great loss. We withdraw from life, wondering, perhaps, if there is any point in going on alone.

ACCEPTANCE
Acceptance is often confused with being "all right". Most people don't ever feel OK about the loss of a loved one. This is about accepting reality that our loved one is physically gone and recognizing that this is the permanent reality. It is the 'new normal' with which we must learn to live. Finding acceptance may be just having more good days than bad.

Meet Brent

"OK, Brent, we'll go through it one more time then it's time for bed." Smiling and shaking my head in pride and amazement, I started the alphabet song with him and let my voice fade as he continued. "A, b, c, d, e, f, g, h, i, j, k, l, m, n, o, p . . ." He always stumbled a little with the "L,

(pictured here at two months)

m, n, o, p" part—kind of ran it together like one word . . . and his little brow would furrow while he looked to me to say it with him, and then he'd smile and finish up with a loud "X, y, and z!" and jump up and give me a hug. It was the best time, really simple yet special. I scooped him up in my arms, praising him, smelling the clean hair and skin from his bath, and feeling the warm pajamas just out of the dryer and tossed him lightly, laughing, onto his bed.

At approximately eighteen months

Why I Want to Be a Pilot

I have wanted to be a pilot for as long as I can remember. Ever since I was a kid I dreamt of flying one sort of aircraft or another. When I was 14, I realized that the best way to get my training was through the military. I decided to do my last three years of high school at New York Military Academy. From there I received a four year Army ROTC scholarship to

Arizona State University. That is where I am now, still working towards my goal of being an officer and a pilot.

I initially wanted to be a fighter pilot in the Air Force. I was really into jets, and thought I would like that. The high school that I went to was an Army based school, and this is where I learned about and fell in love with the Army. I learned all about helicopters and flight training in the Army. I loved the concept of flying attack helicopters, and this dream has not changed to this day.

I geared my schooling in college to course material that I thought could help me achieve this in the future. I started off in Mechanical Engineering, I then found Aeronautical Management Technology, which I changed to last year. I think that this will provide a good background for being a pilot.

To be honest, the main reason that I want to fly is because I am an action junky. I love to do things that get my adrenaline pumping, and I can't think of a better career for someone like myself than being a pilot.

Brent DeLibero, April 1 *(age 20, two months before his death)*

Meet Robbie

I wish I had a picture to show and to keep for myself. Hospitals didn't take pictures of stillborn babies then, and I wasn't thinking ahead enough to ask for one. All I have is this imprint of his tiny feet on the card saying it was a boy. Bob and I both held Robbie after birth, all

wrapped in a light blue blanket—his tiny face looked very much like the baby faces of his older brothers, except for a small triangular mouth from his cleft palate. RIP Robbie.

Meet Brad

It might seem odd to put a picture of my living son Brad in this book about grief, but I'm so proud of him and share a close relationship with him - I wanted you to meet him. Brad Ryan DeLibero is the reason I kept going through all this. He is a bereaved sibling of two brothers, survived the grief, and he is now happy; a successful chef, and a wonderful person. More on his perspective in the book.

Part 1
Brent's Story

Chapter 1

The Phone Call

AS I WALKED into my twenty-one-year-old son Brent's hospital room on that last evening of May, I remember thinking, *How could I be losing another son?* I couldn't believe what I was seeing. My Arizona State University Army ROTC student lay perfectly still, hooked up to life support. Other than all the monitors and tubes, he looked fine, strong and handsome, as if he was just sleeping. I'd lost his younger brother, Robbie, a full-term stillborn son, fifteen years earlier. This couldn't be happening again!

Brent's father, Bob, his younger brother Brad, and I had just gotten off a six-hour-flight in a desperate attempt to get to Arizona before it was too late. Bob had picked up a phone message that morning from Brent's commanding officer, who said that Brent had been in a motorcycle accident, that it was bad, and we should come to Arizona as quickly as we could. Brad, barely nineteen, had just walked into the house after being out all night at his senior prom. It was pure coincidence that they were both at home since neither had planned to be there then. I was on a business trip, having no idea what was happening.

Bob immediately called our good friend Kimm to help. She dropped everything and came right over, making flight arrangements while they packed and got ready to head to Boston's Logan Airport. Bob tried to call my cell phone, and Kimm tried to reach me through my Boston area IBM office, but I was in New Jersey at a customer location.

By chance, I'd stayed with my friend Annette near that customer the night before and had happened to introduce her to my boss, Mike, when we met for a drink. It was good that I did because my cell phone had no reception in the customer's brick building, and only Annette knew exactly where I was. It took them four hours to track me down through my secretary, my boss, my friend, and the company's reception desk. It seemed odd when the meeting room phone rang that someone asked me to take the call.

It was Mike. "Barbara, you need to call Bob right away. I don't know the details," he said, "but I think it's about your son in Arizona." I hung up and tried to reset the phone, fumbling to get an outside line. Finally, Bob picked up. "Thank God," he said when he heard my voice. "I only have a minute . . . they're going to close the airplane door, so I'll have to shut off my phone. Brent has been in a motorcycle accident," he said, "and we need to get to Arizona as fast as we can!"

I felt my stomach drop, something on the way to nausea, and I heard myself utter an involuntary, "No!" a little too loudly. "Oh my God! Is he okay?" "I'm not sure." Bob paused. "But it sounds serious."

This was the nightmare phone call that every parent

dreads, and now that nightmare had come true for me. Suddenly, reality shifted.

"What happened?" I said, my voice tense from fear.

"He was in a motorcycle accident, driving his friend's bike," he replied. "Brad is okay, and he's with me now. We're on our way to the hospital in Scottsdale." He gave me their flight information, which routed through Newark, New Jersey, to Arizona. I managed to tell him that I'd meet them in Newark and find a way to board their flight.

I hung up in tears, informed my associates that there had been an emergency, and that I had to leave. I rushed out of the office, panic rising in my gut. I yelled to a waiting limo driver in the parking lot, asking for the fastest route to Newark airport. Then I jumped into my rental car, trying to memorize the directions he had just given me, and I headed toward the airport, my foot pressing hard on the accelerator. As I drove, I used my cell phone to call Continental Airlines and booked a seat on their flight. But then I ran into heavy New Jersey rush-hour traffic. But it was too early for rush hour, and I realized that there must be an accident somewhere up ahead. I needed to find another route to the airport. "Damn it!" I cursed. My anxiety was rising fast while I felt more helpless by the minute. I called Mike, hoping he could guide me through back roads.

"Mike, I'm so glad I caught you—I need your help."

"I'm glad we found you, I knew something was wrong. What happened?" Hot tears ran down my cheeks, making it hard to see clearly. On top of everything else, I did not need to be in an accident.

"My older son Brent has been in a motorcycle accident," I blurted, "on his campus in Arizona. It's serious. His ROTC commanding officer called to tell us to fly out there. We don't know if he's going to live or die."

I broke down again, crying harder now and choking out the words. "I'm on my way to the airport, and I've run into traffic. Can you help me find another way to Newark so I don't miss my flight?"

Mike stayed on the phone and calmly guided me through an alternative route until I could see signs for the airport.

If I missed that flight, I'd have to make the long trip to Arizona by myself, but worse, this was the last flight of the day from Newark to Phoenix. My stomach was churning. I was not sure if I could make it through the night without seeing Brent. I needed to see Brad, to make sure he was okay and to see how he was coping. I wanted to protect him in any way I could. Of course I also wanted to see Bob, but I'm not sure whether I wanted to protect Bob, draw strength from him, or both. I needed to be with my family!

After what seemed like forever, I made it to the rental car return and got on the tram that circulated between the three large airport terminals at Newark. Then the tram broke down! Palms sweaty, pulse racing, I got out, ran to the next tram to come along, boarded that, and exited at the next stop. It took me a minute to realize that I was in the wrong terminal. *This must be what it feels like to be scared to death*, I thought. I was starting to lose it; my breaths were short and shallow, I could feel myself breaking out in a cold sweat. I waited impatiently for the third tram, and when it arrived, its glass doors sliding open, I jumped aboard. Jesus! Would I miss my flight? In the few minutes I had on the tram, I called my sister Pat, Brent's aunt and godmother, crying while I tried to talk.

I must have looked and sounded hysterical; people were staring at me, but I didn't care. I just wanted everyone out of my way so I could make it to the flight the fastest way possible; I've never been more focused. When I got to the correct terminal, I ran inside, jumped the line in front of someone, apologized, and thrust my ID at the nearest uniformed agent. "I need an urgent boarding pass," I said to her.

"I'm afraid you're on the wrong level," she said. "This one is for international flights. You'll have to go up two levels to check in."

"My son has been in an accident," I shouted, "and he might be dying. I am in danger of missing the last flight to Arizona. Please get me my boarding pass!"

She did.

Now the race to the gate. Of course, the signs indicated that it was the farthest gate from where I stood. In heels and business suit with a straight skirt, I started running, sweating profusely now, carrying my laptop case and dragging my rolling luggage behind me as I approached the security area. "Oh God," I said aloud, thinking, *Will they slow me down?*

"Please help me," I said to the security guard, and then I explained the situation. "Is there a faster way through?"

"Right over there," he said, pointing to the farthest lane against the opposite wall. I could tell from the look in his eyes that he realized how serious this was. But in the shorter line he sent me to, I found myself behind a cursing parent juggling a car seat that he couldn't make fit through the scanner.

"Please," I said. "Let me through!"

He glared at me, mumbled something under his breath, and refused to let me pass. I tried to keep my anger in check as I kept asking myself, *How can this be happening?*

I finally got through. I checked the time on my boarding pass and realized that it was almost time for the flight. My pulse was pounding, I was so scared that I'd miss my flight and my family. Then I noticed a man driving a motorized cart, traveling in the wrong direction. "Wait!" I shouted. "This is an emergency! Can you turn around and take me to my gate?"

He nodded and turned the cart in the opposite direction. "Great!" Thanking him, I breathed a sigh of relief and climbed on, still not sure I'd make it. It was now just ten minutes before the time on my boarding pass, and the airlines usually closed flights fifteen minutes before departure. As we pulled up to my gate, I thanked the driver again, this time through my tears. I grabbed my things, jumped out, and ran to the empty counter. People passing by turned to stare at me.

"Damn! No attending agent!" I said aloud. What was I going to do? Then I realized that there were other people in the gate area. Were they there for the next flight? Or had I missed it? I felt my stomach tighten. Silently, in my head, I screamed, *No!* My stress was becoming so intense, I thought I might explode. I forced myself to take a deep breath and not panic. I needed to think clearly. Confused, I noticed that the Phoenix destination had not yet been removed from the board. Just then, an agent came striding up. I asked the flight status, and he said he was just preparing the boarding process. It was then that I realized I'd been looking at the boarding time, not the flight departure time on my boarding pass—there was still another thirty minutes until departure time, thank God!

I'd made it there a few minutes before my family arrived from Boston. In that moment, I was so relieved that I wanted to kiss that agent! Instead, I tried to calm down while I felt the sweat dripping down my back and hoped it wasn't as obvious as it felt, through my light-colored blouse.

I checked in, dropped my belongings on a chair, and for the next several minutes, paced the floor, waiting for Bob and Brad.

When the three of us finally caught sight of each other, I ran to them and right there in the main aisle, we hugged each other and wept. I can't begin to describe how relieved I was to see them. I could see the stress and pain on Bob's face, and Brad didn't look much better.

We finally boarded the plane for what turned out to be the longest six-hour flight of our lives. The flight attendant, sensing that something was wrong, seated us together in an exit row and handed us water and a box of tissues. For most of the flight, we held on to each other and prayed together for Brent's recovery. I so needed to sit between Bob and Brad where I could physically reach them both.

"It's going to be all right," I kept repeating, and one of them would nod or simply press my hand. "He's going to be okay."

We still didn't know if Brent would make it . . . I do know that Bob or I would have traded our lives for Brent's in an instant. I tried to strike that bargain with God. "Dear, Lord, I'll do anything! Please, don't take Brent away from us!"

While we were in flight, Bob recalled what had happened that morning. Listening was painful and upsetting. So was watching him; his eyes were wet from trying to hold back tears, his face was ashen, and late-day beard stubble had started to appear. My hand was on his arm as he spoke.

"The day started great," he said. "It was my day off. So I got up early, figuring I would get some errands done. The weather was beautiful. I went to get a haircut and came home around 11:00 AM. That's when I got the message from Colonel Crawford asking me to please call him. His exact words were, 'Mr. and Mrs. DeLibero, this is Colonel Crawford, commander of Arizona State University ROTC. Brent was in an accident this morning. Please call as soon as you get this.' Even though he didn't say it was bad or give any details, the message sounded ominous. My heart began to pound. I thought, 'Oh Jesus, please don't let this be bad.'

"My hands were shaking as I dialed the number," Bob continued. "The colonel's wife answered and turned the phone over to him. He got on and he told me as much as he knew: how the motorcycle got away from Brent, how he hit a short cement guard wall and flew more than fifty feet onto a concrete loading dock floor. Shocked, I asked if Brent was okay, and should I come out. He only replied, 'Yes. Come soon.'"

"Jesus," I muttered. "Go on . . . what happened?"

Bob said, "He gave me the name and number of the neurologist who had examined Brent and who wanted to speak with me ASAP. The colonel said I should also call him as soon as we arrived so he could meet us at the hospital. He sounded quite shaken."

Bob continued, "I remember being stunned. Thoughts were starting to swirl around in my head. I felt dizzy, and it was difficult to breathe. I was starting to panic. All I could think about was, My God, I'm going to lose my son, this can't be happening.'"

We held hands as Bob continued telling me the story.

"I tried telling myself they were wrong, that this was all a bad dream. I didn't want to make that call, but I knew I had to. The hospital put me right through to the neurologist. He was very nice, sympathetic. He explained everything that they had observed in Brent during their initial examinations and gave me the results of his medical tests. He described the damage to his leg. I remember hearing most of it, but my mind was flying in every direction. I kept hearing screaming inside my head, 'On my God, oh my God, oh my God!' over and over and over."

I squeezed Bob's hand, tears streaming down my face and asked him to continue. I could feel Brad leaning toward us to hear, and I reached over to grasp my son's hand.

He took a deep breath and looked at me. His eyes were also glistening with tears.

"I asked, 'Is he going to be okay?'" Bob continued. "That's when the realization hit like a bat across my head. His answer was simply, 'I wouldn't hold out much hope. Come as soon as you can.'"

Bob's voice caught as if trying to hold back a sob. "I will *never* forget those words, 'I wouldn't hold out much hope.' I remember wanting to scream at him, 'F——K you! It can't be that cut-and-dried. You assholes missed something! *Fix him!*'"

Bob said he hung up the phone and pounded the counter with his fist. "Dear God," he prayed, "let him be all right. If you have to, take me, but don't take my son! Take me!"

Bob continued, "Then I realized that neither you nor

Brad were home. So I called Brad and left a message saying I needed him to come home or call me as soon as he got the message. I tried calling you but got no answer. I called your office in Waltham, asking if they had a way to reach you other than your cell, and they said they would try. Then I called my boss and told him what happened and that I was flying out to Arizona. I was still holding it together, but my voice was cracking. I ran upstairs to throw some clothes into a suitcase for me and Brad. Then I called my father, he said, 'Oh, Jesus Christ, Bob, I'm sorry.' and I could hear him crying. I told him I didn't know how to do this, if I even could. He encouraged me to be strong and to keep him and my sister posted. Finally, I heard our front door open and Brad called upstairs to me. I asked if he had gotten my message, and he said no. He must have sensed something in my voice because he ran up the stairs, came into the room, took one look at me, and asked what was wrong. I told him Brent had been in an accident, and they didn't think he would make it."

'What the F——K!' he said. Then he fell onto my shoulder and cried. We stood like that for a minute when it finally hit me full force. I ran into the bathroom, grabbed a towel, and began screaming into it. I couldn't stop. I was bent over, face buried in the towel. I felt Brad's hand on my shoulder as he tried to comfort me.

"I called our friend Kimm for help, and by the time she arrived, she'd called another friend, Kyle, and he was looking up flights online. They got my info, knew you were in New Jersey, and booked a flight through Newark. Brad and I rushed to the airport.

"When I explained what had happened, a Continental employee helped us move through the lines. My voice was cracking, and she began crying as she helped us. We got on the plane, same row but different sides of the aisle. I held Brent's picture in my hand and kept looking at it. Just then, I got your call and gave you our flight, I was relieved that they'd reached you. Brad, from his seat, asked if we were going to meet you in New Jersey, and if the doctors were going to meet us in Arizona. I nodded yes to both questions. The guy next to me saw the picture and overheard our conversation. He asked if we wanted to sit together, but we both said no thanks. I think we needed our own space. But I was worried about Brad and kept looking over at him. Suddenly, we ran into a storm and hit the worst turbulence I had ever felt, even worse than when I was in the air force. Everybody was worried. The plane was bouncing so hard. Brad looked over at me as if to say, 'What the hell!' I thought, 'This can't be real.' Brent is dying, and now we are too. Then I thought, 'maybe that's how it should be.' I just looked at Brad, tears streaming down my face."

As Bob and I sat holding on to each other, he stopped talking, exhausted. We were quiet for a few minutes; then Brad began to talk. He also had a powerful recollection of what he'd felt that morning. His high school senior prom had been the night before.

"I got back from the prom," he said, "dropped my date off and went to the café for breakfast." He worked there part-time; the café was located diagonally across from our home. "After breakfast, I came home to find Dad taking socks out of my drawer, packing. I asked what was going on. Dad told me what happened, and that he was flying out to Arizona.

"'Should I come?' I asked him. 'How bad is it? Is he OK?'

"'Yes,' Dad said, 'you should come. We don't know if Brent's going to make it.'

"I was shocked, my eyes filled up, and then I went quiet because I didn't want to make it worse for Dad. I tried to figure out how I could help, because it was obvious that he was in a hurry. I remember that no one could reach you, Mom, but we had to go. I remember feeling that we had to play the cards we were dealt.

"Within twenty or thirty minutes, Dad and I were on the way to the airport. I called work to tell them that I wouldn't be in and why. Once we got to the airport," Brad continued, "it took forever to get through security. I don't remember anything about the short flight to Newark. I must have been in shock. The next thing I remember is meeting you at the gate in Newark then us getting on this flight. I felt so out of it. I mostly remember hearing Dad's voice saying over and over that Brent might not make it." Brad paused, looked down then continued—tears starting to leak out of the corners of his eyes. "I am really afraid of what I might see when we walk into Brent's hospital room, but I think I am more afraid of what would happen if Brent doesn't make it—what will I do then?"

I felt so badly for Brad, but I had no answer for him. I could only hold his hand and try not to think about having to live without Brent.

We finally got to Phoenix, an enormous and complex airport, where we were met with another set of obstacles. We could not find the friend who was supposed to pick us up, nor could we reach him by phone. We later learned that he'd been there, but we didn't connect because we were on different levels of the same terminal.

Growing more frantic, I hailed the first limo I saw and asked him to take us to Scottsdale Osborne Trauma Center as fast as possible. We climbed in and en route, there was confusion about how to pay him: cash, which we hadn't taken the time to obtain, or credit card, which he wasn't set up to accept. More time wasted to sort it out in our desperate effort to get to Brent. Every second was precious.

The limo driver must have thought we were crazy—we begged him to speed all the way there. We had no idea whether Brent was still hanging on waiting for us, or if he might die any minute.

After what felt like an endless thirty-minute drive, we walked into the waiting room outside Brent's hospital room in the intensive care unit (ICU) area filled with his friends, commanding officer, and ROTC buddies.

They said Laura and her parents were in Brent's room with him. Laura was a lovely young woman that Brent met and fell in love with while at ASU. She was blond, slender and athletic, intelligent and quiet, with a lovely personality. Laura and Brent had plans to get married just after he graduated from college and before he began active army duty thirty days later. They'd recently told us that they were signing papers on an apartment to move in together the following month.

Brent had a part-time job and was saving for an engagement ring. I'd supposed he was going to pop the question soon. We already considered Laura and her parents part of our family; we loved Laura.

We greeted everyone in the waiting area briefly but didn't

waste any time getting let through the big double doors to be shown into his room on the right, near the nurse's station in the ICU. The young man whose motorcycle Brent had driven introduced himself, and he looked terribly upset. I remember him apologizing, but I didn't know for what. I noticed that my cousin from Scottsdale was there with my aunt, who was visiting from Nebraska. I thought that vaguely odd but didn't want to take the time to think about why they would be there or how they found out. Some of these people had been there all day, and they looked exhausted as if they'd been holding a vigil for Brent while waiting for us. I just hugged them and moved on—so many people to get through. I appreciated their support, but all I could think about was getting to my son—I needed to hold him!

But I was afraid of what I'd find. Was he in pain? Was his body mangled? Would he recognize us or even be conscious? Would he live? Would he be impaired? Would he still be able to be a pilot? He'd be so disappointed if he couldn't fly since he'd wanted to be a pilot since he was fifteen, but we'd help him get through it if he just lived! Knowing my virile, athletic son, I was afraid he wouldn't want to live if he were severely handicapped. I was already feeling the loss of the future he had planned with Laura and his career. *Let me just see him and how bad it is.*

In hindsight, seeing Laura and her parents at Brent's bed was very telling, but it didn't sink in at the time. Laura was at his bedside, looking so hurt and exhausted. Her eyes were red and swollen, filled with tears, her long blond hair falling over her slumped shoulders. Her parents were there too, looking worried. They got up to hug us. Then my aunt and cousin followed us in, hugged us, and stepped to the side. There were several nurses in and out, greeting us, and saying they would get the doctor. It seemed like a lot of people in one room; but at least he was in a private room.

It was hard to see him all hooked up to tubes, but he had a peaceful look on his handsome face, only his usual warm smile was missing. I was surprised that he didn't look that bad. It was as though he was only sleeping. I kissed his forehead, hugged him, and told him I loved him. I stepped out of the way to let Bob and Brad make contact with Brent while I started to check out his injuries. He was in the best shape I'd ever seen him—really physically fit, finally having achieved his "six pack" abs that he'd been striving for. Other than a small scratch on his forehead and a dark red spot under the Band-Aid on his neck where he'd been intubated at the scene, there was no evidence of an accident. Maybe he'd be okay.

I realized I was talking to him softly, like he was awake, and I was trying to comfort him but find out how he was without violating his privacy. I lifted the sheet gingerly and saw his badly swollen and purple right knee and leg. I winced, it looked so painful—but still, not bad enough to kill him. Good.

He's strong. He's athletic and healthy, I told myself. He'll be okay. "Pull yourself out of this, Brent—you always do."

I'd been in the emergency room with this kid and his brother more times than I could count! He'd survived many broken bones, concussions, stitches, and other traumas; surely he would survive this. But it bothered me that he wasn't moving.

I'd expected him to be so mangled that I'd steeled myself, but other than his painful-looking knee, he didn't look scraped up at all. What the hell was going on? Doctors are not perfect, right? They could be wrong. I tried talking to Brent, my voice getting louder, trying to make him stir.

"Wake up, Brent! Dad, Brad, and I are here. You're going to be okay! Fight, dammit! You've survived so many accidents and broken bones before, you can survive this too! We'll help you, no matter what it takes."

My love pats became small slaps and pinches; my voice louder now. Could I snap him into consciousness? They *must* be wrong! All the while my heart was telling me to keep on hoping, that he was somehow going to make it. Yet my intuition was screaming that he was not going to make it. *Can he hear me?* I wondered even if it was only via his subconscious. *Does he know we're here? Can he feel how much we love him?*

"Wake up, damn it!" I said. He gave no indication of hearing me; he didn't stir.

I turned to hug Laura; she looked so drained, so tired. She loved him so much, and fear was all over her face. No wonder; she faced the possibility of living the rest of her life without her best friend, partner, and lover. I wanted to tell her it was all right, but of course I couldn't. I hated feeling so helpless.

"What happened?" I finally asked her.

Laura said that Brent had been leaving before dawn every morning for his ROTC physical training. But today, he was able to get up a little earlier, giving himself a few extra minutes that he wouldn't normally have. When ready to go, he climbed back into bed on her side and gave her a hug and kiss. "I felt so much love from him," she said. "Then he left, and I never suspected that these were the last minutes we would have together."

She went to work that morning at her college internship. Excited that it was Friday, she was the first person to arrive at work.

She glanced at her cell and noticed that a call had come in from Brent's phone. She listened to the voicemail on the way into the lobby. It wasn't Brent; it was one of his good ROTC friends, Ryan, that she also knew well, asking her to call back as soon as she could.

Feeling something was terribly wrong, Laura sat down at the receptionist's desk right inside the doorway and returned the call. "There's been an accident," Ryan said. "Go straight to the hospital."

Laura was scared and now wondered how she drove to the hospital on her own. A police officer arrived a few minutes later, saying he'd been involved at the accident scene, had gotten off duty, and wanted to come check on Brent. He told her we'd already been contacted and were on our way. He also suggested that she call someone who could get there quickly, like her parents, for support. It was at that moment that she realized how bad it was; that Brent might not be coming home with her.

"I just wanted to see Brent," she told me now. "I didn't know if he'd be conscious or not. I remember getting to his floor and seeing his friends who'd been at the accident scene. They all had long faces; it was obvious they'd been crying, and I thought I was about to walk into a living hell, which is exactly what it was. I remember noticing three things: first, there was only a scratch on his forehead; second, he had tubes going into his throat; and third, his chest was moving in rhythm with the machine, so I knew he wasn't breathing on his own. It was worse than I thought."

REFLECTION:

In hindsight, it now seems clear to me that what I experienced, very powerfully, was essentially a normal reaction to a traumatic event. I was shocked, terrified, and yet numb all at the same time. It felt like I'd entered into a surreal part of my life for which I wasn't prepared.

The day had started normally, but when the phone call came, suddenly, time stopped. I felt stuck, suspended in a kind of jail that I wanted to escape but could not. I wanted proof that this was really happening, yet at the same time, I did not want confirmation that my son was dying. I remember thinking this can't be happening. This must be a dream. There's got to be a way to turn the clock back and start this day over.

Of course, this is a classic example of the <u>denial</u> *phase. Even Laura was in denial when she assumed Brent could call her or would return home with her that day. It's human to expect a good ending.*

For me, during the initial impact and my <u>denial</u>*, I began to enter into the next phase;* <u>bargaining</u>*. Both Bob and I would have readily traded our lives for Brent's, if we'd been able to. We tried. I'm guessing that even Brad did that or promised God that he would do something big if his brother lived; he is so unselfish. Even while I was trying to* <u>bargain</u> *with God, I was actually starting into an* <u>acceptance</u> *of the initially inconceivable idea that my son might be dying.*

I'd stopped practicing formal religion much earlier, and I didn't think of myself as spiritual. Yet instinctively, I reached out to God for help, falling back on my religious Catholic tradition through the prayers I'd learned as a child.

I experienced an immediate and palpable <u>anger</u> that was situational and differed from the kind of <u>anger</u> and even rage that I went through later in the grief process. In those early moments, I was frustrated at anyone or anything that kept me from getting to my son's side. Soon, I was angry with my son for being careless, and even God for letting this happen, but I now see that was another normal stage in this journey.

Chapter 2

The Hospital

NOW THAT I had seen him and realized he was still living, I needed to find out more about the accident and how my son got to the hospital. I began by asking Laura and his friends about it. They said that after Brent had passed his ROTC physical training test, and the guys decided to go to breakfast less than a mile down the road, near the ASU campus. Although Brent had his own car there, his buddy Oz, showed up that morning with a brand-new one-week-old "rice rocket": a powerful Honda 950 motorcycle. That is a racing bike, too dangerous for anyone but the most experienced rider.

Brent had told us of his interest in motorcycles when we took him to Las Vegas, just three weeks earlier, to celebrate his twenty-first birthday. We'd been standing in front of the MGM Grand Hotel on the Las Vegas Strip when a guy pulled up on a motorcycle. He was not wearing a helmet. We expressed our concerns about the wisdom of that, whether the state required one or not. Arizona and Nevada had no helmet law.

Brent told us that he had been test-driving motorcycles and hoped to save for one. He had not yet gotten his permit; his only experience with them was an occasional drive on a much less powerful bike in the relative safety of a motorcycle dealers' lot. As far as we knew, he'd never driven a motorcycle on public streets.

We'd been trying to discourage his interest in motorcycles, pointing out the dangers. But he was twenty-one, living two thousand miles from home, and free to do what he wanted with his own money. Although we had helped with his college expenses, we purposely did not give him enough for extras like that. But he decided he wanted one badly enough to get a part-time job as a waiter, intending to save for an engagement ring for Laura—and for a motorcycle.

We were delighted about the ring, but we hated that he wanted a motorcycle, knowing that once he'd set a goal, our son was a risk taker and tenacious. But Brent promised us that even if he did buy a motorcycle, he wouldn't get on one without a helmet. He understood that driving without one was dangerous. Yet he wasn't wearing one when he had this accident. I wondered sadly, "Why not?"

We learned from Brent's friends that Oz lived near the site of that morning's physical training, and he was a very experienced rider, using some form of motorized cycle since he was seven years old. He'd not bothered to wear his helmet that morning. He rode the short distance from home without it, thinking he was the only one who would be using his bike. However, Brent talked Oz into letting him drive his brand-new motorcycle to breakfast. After all, it was only a short distance, so what could go wrong? For some reason, Oz believed that Brent had his motorcycle license, even though he admitted to me that he had not asked him directly. Oz also said that Brent didn't lie about it, they just didn't discuss it. I wish they had. Maybe my son would still be alive. But Brent was a very confident and persuasive young man. He'd been successful at many things in his life and must have been excited at the opportunity to try that shiny new machine. At twenty-one, I imagine he felt "invincible," not thinking much about the danger involved.

But in one fateful moment, he handed his car keys to Oz, and they switched vehicles. The story I heard was that Brent started the bike and drove it out of the ASU parking lot, but at the stop sign on that nearby corner, it stalled. I'm guessing that this might have embarrassed him in front of his ROTC buddies. He restarted the engine, and as he made the right turn to head to breakfast, he began to lose control of the heavy machine. When it nearly tipped over, Brent tried to accelerate to regain control. He could have cut the power, which might have damaged the bike and perhaps his leg, but instead, he chose to try save the bike and lost his life. I'll never know what he was thinking, or maybe he wasn't thinking at all. Maybe it was just his reflexes, or maybe he was saving face, but I'd give anything if I could rewind that moment and make him lay that bike down. Brent swerved in a diagonal across McAllister Avenue, over the curb, and onto the lawn of the ASU Ross-Blakely Law library as his friends watched helplessly. Brent lost control of the powerful motorcycle while still on the ASU campus.

The library was an odd-looking oval building, resembling a dusty gray elongated metal igloo. In front of it was a sparse lawn, similar to many lawns in desert areas. To the right of the building was a cement loading dock with a wide ramp, enclosed by a U-shaped cement wall and vertical barrier about three feet high, with sloping sides leading to an off-the-street truck entrance.

Later, the police report would describe the accident in more detail. We know that Brent accelerated right into that loading dock wall in front of the ASU Law library, slamming into the wall, and crushing his knee against it. He'd been going fast enough for the bike to take two chunks out of the cement wall.

The momentum threw Brent over that wall on to the loading dock below. He landed fifty-six feet away, his head hitting the cement ramp. The force of the impact was tremendous; they found his sneaker more than twenty feet from the point of impact, in the opposite direction from which he'd been traveling. Although Brent's bare and unprotected head took the impact, the momentum kept his body moving in a cartwheel until he rolled to a stop.

His friends said it looked like he may have pulled back on the handlebars, hoping to slow the bike. But instead, he sped it up, making his landing more violent. I have only a meager knowledge of motorcycle controls, but the mechanism for managing speed had always seemed counterintuitive to me, so I could understand what they were saying. Or perhaps the centrifugal force of the acceleration pulled him off the bike as it sped up, resulting in him instinctively holding on to avoid falling off—tightening his grip on the accelerator and increasing his speed. We'll never know. I imagined the panic he must have felt at the end, and I prayed he hadn't felt pain. What started out as an adventure for him went horribly wrong.

Shocked and horrified, his friends called 911; and within

three minutes, the ASU Police and emergency ambulance were on the scene. They intubated Brent so that he could breathe, and they rushed him to the Scottsdale Osborne Trauma Center. Because ASU is such a large school, with nearly fifty thousand students on their one-mile-square Tempe campus, they have their own police department and infrastructure, like any city of that size might. Because the accident occurred within a block of the campus police station, they were able to respond quickly.

Sitting in his hospital room, gazing down at my son, I found myself thinking, *Damn young men who think they are invincible!* While I loved Brent and feared that he was dying, still I was angry at him for getting on a motorcycle he had no business being on. I was also angry at the possibility of losing him. Could God really be taking two of my three sons? Was that possible or even imaginable? And . . . if he did, could I survive it?

I was beginning to understand that it *was* possible, and I needed to try to prevent it if I could.

"Wake up, Brent!" I said aloud while I was thinking, *Do it for me, for your father! Do it for the grandchildren you're supposed to give us! Do it for your brother! Your brother, damn it!"*

But Brent didn't move, didn't flinch, gave no sign that he'd heard me.

I looked at Brad, standing beside Brent's bed. Younger by just two years, it was clear that he was crushed to see his older brother in this state. Brad wasn't small, standing at six feet tall with broad shoulders. But at this moment, he looked so helpless, so young and scared. I wanted to do something to protect him from all this somehow. I was used to making things happen, to being in control. I hated feeling helpless.

For a moment, I turned from Brent to put my arms around Brad. He just stood there, slumped, head down, limp and nearly lifeless himself. He was hurting for his brother and probably feeling as sad and helpless as I was.

Later, Brad told me that in these moments, he had felt helpless, but also hopeful, like his brother was going to suddenly open his eyes, sit up, and somehow be okay. Brad felt angry too, not at anyone in particular, he said. But he felt strongly that the accident should not have happened, that Brent was too young. He was right.

During this time, Bob was standing on the other side of Brent's bed, with his hand on Brent's arm, leaning over him, occasionally whispering to him. Bob was clearly in tremendous emotional pain. I walked over and put my arms around my husband. He just shook his head no and said, "This isn't possible. It can't be happening." He could barely speak.

I remember thinking that Bob didn't look any better than Brad; he looked worse if that were possible. His relationship with Brent was strong and deep. They had similar interests and did many things together; they even looked and walked alike. Some of their shared interests included sports, especially baseball, and theater. They'd performed in plays together and even wrote poetry together. For a jock and someone who loved the military, Brent made good use of his creative side. He'd taken drawing lessons with me too; he liked doing portrait sketches.

I moved between despair and hope, trying to think positively and not let myself believe that Brent might be dying. I have always been action-oriented and desperately tried to think of something I could *do* to make any of this better. I was also fighting off the terrible sinking feeling that this time, I might not be able to fix things.

Eight of us stood in his hospital room now, talking to Brent, watching over, and praying for him. One of his doctors, a neurosurgeon, entered the room, introduced himself, and offered his sympathies. I remember feeling that it seemed too casual, too practiced, not really heartfelt.

"Would you come with me please?" he said.

I'd been dreading this moment ever since the phone call, the trip through the airport, during the flight to Arizona, and in the car on the way to the trauma center. I'd dreaded this moment while greeting Brent's friends and even as I hugged Brent, checked him for signs of injury, and saw the effect on his father, his brother, and his fiancée.

The doctor beckoned to everyone in Brent's room to follow him. It seemed like there were too many of us for an intimate discussion; it annoyed me.

Bob, Brad, Laura and her parents, my cousin, my aunt, and I all followed him down a long hall, along with hospital staff who I later realized were the head ICU nurse on duty and the hospital chaplain. We eventually ended up in a very large brightly lit room with a long conference table. This impromptu journey didn't seem well thought out. As we walked along, the doctor stuck his head into a couple of other rooms that seemed not to his liking or already occupied. It reminded me of a last-minute corporate meeting when we'd forgotten to schedule a conference room and were scrambling to find a suitable place fast. It struck me that the doctor wanted to get the meeting over as quickly as possible and be done with it.

Of course, I was still hoping he would give us an update and options for helping Brent recover. Surely there must be something that could be done! Brent was in amazing shape. I realized that it might take a long time for him to recover, and he might have to give up his dream of becoming a Comanche or Apache helicopter pilot. But surely somehow his life could be saved, and then we would help him make progress, however slow.

But there was something about the demeanor of this doctor that made me uneasy. His movements were a little too quick, too matter-of-fact, too much like he'd already decided something.

He entered the room and seated himself and his staff at one end of a ridiculously long conference table. He motioned for Bob, Brad, Laura, and me to sit at the far end and casually directed the others to sit on the chairs along the wall. I felt like there was a mile of table between us and the staff. It all felt so distant, so cold and unreal.

I feared he was about to deliver the worst possible news, but then I told myself that he wouldn't do that in this sterile bright room, seated so far from us, with so many other people around, would he? He must be preparing to give us an update or suggest an action plan.

I looked around at the others, and while I didn't know what they were thinking, everyone was avoiding my eyes, avoiding looking at me and the doctor. I hated this sterile room, this distant doctor—everything about this!

I was feeling dazed, running on fumes after a long stressful day. Yet I was hopeful, we'd arrived only fifteen minutes earlier, after all. It seemed much longer than that—this painful, sad experience of finding our older son unconscious, attached to tubes and machines.

Brent was my jock, my athlete, the one who seemed to play or at least try every sport known to man. He was always vibrant and in control. How could that young man I'd just seen be my Brent? Was he in there somewhere, fighting for himself? Was anyone at this hospital fighting for him?

We all sat down, and I fixed my gaze intently on the doctor, anxiously waiting for what he had to say. I wanted to hear every word. I remember thinking, *This man has my child's life in his hands*.

Then the doctor began to speak. "I'm sorry," he said, looking at each of us in turn. "Your son suffered a terrible head injury. We did everything we could. He was declared brain-dead three hours ago. There's nothing more we can do."

Completely stunned, I remained silent, unable to speak, unable to stop the tears streaming down my face. Reality had shifted again; nothing made sense. I felt like I must not have heard the doctor correctly even though I knew I had. I felt in shock, like someone had punched me so hard in the stomach, and I could not breathe. When I finally looked at Bob and Brad, they too looked physically crushed—bodies slumped, faces ashen. Laura looked like she might collapse. Without realizing it, I reached out for them. My insides were caving in on themselves. I was suddenly empty and profoundly sad in a way that I'd never before experienced. But then the natural numbness began that would help to protect me like a suit of armor.

But no matter how I felt, I knew I would need to show strength for my family, Bob and I both would. And we would need to be as much of an advocate for Brent as we could.

I think part of me knew what the doctor was going to say before he said it. Even after he had said that Brent was brain-dead, part of me was still hoping and praying that there was a chance Brent could survive. Even when I'd seen the faces of his friends outside his hospital room, I'd thought, I won't give up. There's got to be a way to save him.

The doctor continued, saying that Brent's head trauma was too severe. His brain had swollen and cut off oxygen to his brain stem. This could not be fixed or healed. Brent would not recover. He shared this information quickly, without much softening or sympathy. Just the facts delivered emotionlessly in this sterile bright room. I didn't detect much compassion; it felt surreal.

But my mind flashed back to a six-year-old Brent. He was yelling, "Hey, Mom!" It was not long since we'd moved into our newly built home in a new neighborhood full of families with children. I went to the front door to see why he was calling me, and then I saw him on his bike, rolling fast down the steep driveway of the unfinished neighbor's house. He was standing on the bicycle's crossbar, and he wasn't holding on! He had a huge smile on his face, and all I could do was hold my breath until he made it to the end of the driveway.

And now this. The Brent that I remembered couldn't be the son I had just seen hooked up to life support.

We'd hardly begun to absorb the tragic news when the chaplain, who looked like a kindly grandmother, seated at the other end of this long table, interrupted our thoughts and personal conversation to ask if we wanted to donate Brent's organs! It was as if she'd slapped me. Her timing struck me as untimely, if not cruel.

I remember blinking through my tears, hardly believing what I'd just heard. She wanted to cut my son's body open! I understood that an organ donation would help others, and Brent was probably an ideal candidate, but we needed time to think about it, to sleep on it.

I finally found the voice to say that.

"But it should be done tonight," the head nurse responded.

I shook my head. Why was she rushing us? It was already 9:00 PM local time, midnight on our body clocks, and we were exhausted on so many levels. I thought I knew what this was about; they didn't want to waste another day of the hospital facilities on someone who had no chance of recovery. They wanted to harvest his organs and remove him from life support as soon as possible, free up the room. Of course, she didn't say it quite that bluntly, but I guessed that was what she meant.

How stupid and callous these people seemed. Had they been hardened from dealing with so much death? While their intentions may have been good, they seemed to give no real consideration to the shock we were in or the sorrow we felt. I felt my anger rising, and then I went ballistic. "Are you crazy?!? I can't believe you people! This is our *son* that you just told us is *dead*! Do you have *any* feelings at all?" It was hard trying to speak through my own rage and grief.

I was so angry; it felt like I was walking up one side of that doctor's body and down the other, wearing sharp spiked heels. My family knows not to get in my way when I'm that angry, especially when I'm being protective of them. These people seemed unprepared for my reaction. How dare this doctor and his staff try to dispose of my son without even giving us time to absorb the truth—that we had just lost him?

"You're not getting near our son!" I said. "Not until we've

had time with him. And after my sister arrives tomorrow afternoon."

I stood up. The doctor, the nurse, and the chaplain just stared at me.

"And do not take him off life support," I said. "Not until we've had a chance to talk as a family. We just got here. We also want a second opinion on his condition and his options."

The doctor blinked as though taken aback, but then he nodded and mumbled something about being sorry.

"We'll arrange for his other neurologists to speak with you in the morning," he said.

We stood up, hugged each other again, and got out of there as fast as we could, clinging to each other on the way out. We were weeping; Laura's parents were flanking her. My cousin and aunt were shaking their heads in disbelief. We all headed back to spend the time we had left with Brent.

REFLECTION:

During this time, I was experiencing so many feelings. They were jumbled, and they came fast and furiously. The thick numbness didn't last long, and after a while, it did little to hide my growing depression. *There were periods of growing* anger *too. I wasn't always sure what these feelings meant or whom to direct them at, but it included* anger *at the manufacturers of the motorcycle. It seemed to me that what was really a racing bike was being sold for use on city streets, targeting a market of young men looking for excitement. Laws and regulations protect us against self-harm in so many ways, why were there no laws to govern these bikes? Companies should not be making a profit on products that hurt and kill our children.*

I was still somewhat in <u>denial</u> about Brent while starting to <u>accept</u> this worst possible outcome. But I also realized how futile it was to try to control older children. They understand fairly early on when the time comes that parents no longer have any real control over them, and they can do what they want to do. If a risky hobby is within their means and if they are daring enough, they'll probably pursue it.

We'd raised Brent to be independent and a risk taker, thinking those qualities would be important for him in adulthood. Even in hindsight, I would not have changed that about him, nor would I have done anything but try to help him have a full, adventurous life. He packed a lot of living into his short life; no regrets there. But I was surprised at my <u>anger</u> at his being careless, not considering the impact to everyone around him. I was also disappointed that he broke his promise never to ride on a motorcycle without a helmet.

In the years after this accident, in my work with other bereaved parents, I've noticed that frequently, it seems that the child they lose is one who's packed the most into his or her short life, almost though they sense subconsciously that their life will end early.

My <u>denial</u> continued; I was still questioning, still hoping that he might be wrong—doctors were fallible, right? We sought out second opinion and insisted on understanding the scans and detailed test results before anything final was done

I was <u>angry</u> at the cool, "professional" way they treated us and Brent, like he was just another "faceless" case. They'd tried to be nice and even, at times, somewhat sympathetic. But they did not handle us with the care that any newly bereaved parent should be given. *No one can fully understand the deep impact of being told your child has died without having experienced it.* Hospital staff deal with death so much, they probably have to grow somewhat callous to withstand the constant barrage of pain they would otherwise experience.

But I believe that sensitivity training is needed for emergency, trauma, health care, and funeral professionals in dealing with families who have lost a child of any age. If that can make it a little easier for even one parent to move through this ordeal, then it's worth it.

I think that Brent's friend Oz, for a long time, went through variations of <u>anger, denial, and depression</u>. Brent was very persuasive and overconfident while Oz may have been too casual about lending his buddy such a dangerous motorcycle. Initially, I was angry at both of them until later, when I realized that neither of them could foresee such a tragic outcome. It was just a stupid mistake by two young men, buddies. At that age, we don't think about our own mortality.

Over the years, I'm sure Oz has replayed that moment in his head many times. I accepted his role and forgave him, feeling it was primarily Brent's fault as he could talk almost anyone into anything. But Brent had an amazing future planned and would not have put his family and Laura through all this pain on purpose. I don't think any of our children do.

Later on, I would hear from Oz's friends that he was <u>depressed</u> after the accident. I did speak with him in that year following the accident, making sure he knew that I didn't hold him responsible. I'd love to talk to him again, but I don't know how to reach him. Before we *left Arizona, though, I did extract a promise from him and Brent's other friends: never to get on a motorcycle without a helmet. In a small way, their promises help me feel that this tragedy might have prevented one for someone else.*

I think Bob struggled more with the <u>anger</u> in many areas than I did, maybe partly from a dad's perspective. The grief stages and their sequence are very personally unique.

Chapter 3

Tough Decisions

ONCE WE TOLD the doctor of our intention to wait until family had gathered—and made it clear that we planned to spend the night—there was nothing more we could accomplish. We left the conference room, shaking our heads in disbelief, and headed back to Brent's room, which thankfully allowed us the space we needed. Bob and I held hands, but neither of us was saying much. I looked over at him and asked, "Are you okay?" He just shrugged and nodded. Brad walked close to us with his head down, quiet.

No one could have pried us out of Brent's room. Even if we weren't sure Brent could hear us, we needed to believe that he could. As much as we hated to think about it and as badly as the hospital staff had handled the situation, we understood we had to make a decision regarding organ donation. I said to Bob, "We have a lot to talk about. Let's say good-bye to the others and decide about organ donation with Brad and Laura." We said good-bye to my cousin and aunt, hugged them, thanked them for their support then we went out to the waiting area briefly to update Brent's friends and let them know it was all right to go home and get some rest.

Later, we learned that hospitals designate motorcycle riders as "organ donors" because motorcycle accidents often result in head injuries and brain death, leaving the other organs undamaged and viable for harvest.

The thought of cutting my son open was so painful; it would not be an easy decision. We needed to spend more time with Brent—touch him, tell him how much we loved him, and comfort each other. We had to make a decision, but doing so implied that we were giving up. Was it too soon? I remember praying, "Dear, God, please let Brent wake up!"

Bob, Brad, Laura, and I gathered around Brent's bed to try to decide what to do. Their faces were pale; they didn't want to be part of this decision any more than I did. Brent had never expressed an interest in organ donation. Neither had he identified himself as an organ donor on his driver's license. What we did know about him was that he was deeply proud of his affiliation with the army, and we were equally proud of his ambition to serve. If there were to be a funeral, he would be in his army dress uniform in an open casket. We wanted family and friends to be able to see him, touch him, and say good-bye. We worried that harvesting his organs would make that impossible.

It felt as though the procedure would cause him more pain and trauma, although logically, we knew that was unlikely. I heard the pain in Bob, Brad, and Laura's voices during our discussion. It was clear to me that they didn't want to do it.

"What do you think we should do?" I said.

Bob looked at me. "I don't want him cut up," he said.

Brad and Laura nodded in agreement, looking down at their folded hands resting on the edge of Brent's bed.

I remember thinking, *They should not have to be making a decision like this. None of us should.* Part of me wanted to go ahead with the donation, knowing that Brent would live on in others, but I had to respect their wishes. I could not cause any of us more pain.

"Okay. We'll decline the hospital's request," I said.

Laura went to tell her parents of our decision.

Laura and her wonderful parents, Maureen and Larry, had been standing vigil since Brent arrived at the hospital before 8:00 AM that day. I was moved by this and their strong support of everyone present. We'd become instant friends from the moment we met over dinner in Arizona earlier, and especially so once we understood that Brent and Laura were in love.

They'd been so very nice to Brent, and it was obvious that they loved him like we loved Laura. We had welcomed this new relationship with Brent's future in-laws. It could not have been more perfect.

Even as we grappled with the loss of Brent, I recognized the possibility that we would also be losing Laura and her parents as potential in-laws and friends. I worried how they, in turn, would be affected by Brent's death; he was a big part of their lives and quite a presence.

But that was too much to think about just then.

Laura, emotionally and physically exhausted, decided she needed to go home and get some rest so that she could return in the morning. She felt better about leaving knowing we were going to spend the night with Brent. We embraced, and she left with her parents.

I had seen the concern in Maureen's and Larry's faces, compassion for us, grief at losing their future son-in-law, hurt in seeing Laura suffer—all compounded by their worry about how she would handle all this going forward. She'd lost a good friend not long before and was finally starting to move on. I felt so badly for Laura who was seeing her future vanish before her eyes. Just like I was; a future with Brent and the adventure that always surrounded him, a future with her children and my grandchildren, a future that bonded us together as in-laws and family. I wished I could make it better somehow—for her, for Brad, for Bob, for her parents, for Brent's friends . . . even for myself.

As we spent our last hours with Brent, we found it hard to let go of the hope that this was just a nightmare we'd wake up from. But he remained motionless in his hospital bed, still hooked to tubes and wires to help him breathe, hydrate him, and monitor his vital signs. It was unbelievable, just unbelievable.

Bob, Brad and I surrounded Brent's bed, Bob with his head in one hand and his other hand on Brent's arm. Brad, on the other side up near Brent's pillow, was unable to take his eyes off his brother. I was still looking for any signs of life. Then something happened—his foot moved.

"Brent," I said, "can you hear me? Can you hear *us*?" Nothing. No response. No more movement. No sign that he heard us. I sat and watched his feet and a few minutes later, it happened again. *Oh my God! Maybe there's hope*, I thought.

"Did you see that?" I said, looking from Brad to Bob.

Brad had seen it too.

"He moved," he said. There was a look of hope on his face as he moved around to the end of the bed with me. He laid his hand gently on one of Brent's feet. A nurse came in to check on him, and we asked her about it. She looked genuinely sad as she told us that because of chemical changes in his body, his muscles were contracting involuntarily. She said that she was sorry, but we should not take it as an indication that he was recovering. He had no brain activity.

I didn't want to believe her. I wanted to believe that somehow, Brent was going to prove them all wrong, beat all the odds, and recover. I wanted to scream at her, "'You're wrong, he's going to pull through this!"

But in the pit of my stomach, I knew she was right. Still, I wasn't ready to give up yet. I reminded her that we'd asked for a second opinion.

It was too late tonight, but I asked her to arrange for another trauma center neurologist to speak with us in the morning. I hadn't heard from the other doctor. We couldn't just take one doctor's word on something so grave, so final about our son.

Just then the hospital chaplain came in. "Have you made a decision yet?" she asked. She looked hopeful.

I looked at Bob and Brad, who were both naturally quiet, and understood, as usual, that I had to be the one to answer.

"We've decided not to donate Brent's organs," I said. "It was a difficult decision. This was all too sudden." I told her we hadn't time to absorb it.

"I'm sorry," I said. "We realize that a donation could help others, but we're in too much shock to make a quick decision, and there is no time.

"Besides that, we have to allow our family time to see him one last time and say good-bye, and we need to afford him the dignity of being waked in his army uniform with an open casket."

The chaplain looked very disappointed. "Are you sure, Mr. and Mrs. DeLibero?" as she looked at us with a pleading expression.

"Yes, we've talked it over. We're sure," I replied. Bob confirmed with a nod and a quiet "Yes".

Finally, she accepted our decision—reluctantly, it seemed to us—and left the room.

By now it was late locally, and our bodies were still operating on Eastern time. To us, it was the middle of the night, and we were bone-tired. We couldn't bear to leave Brent and looked for a way to spend the night at the hospital. There were a couple of couches and a recliner chair in the waiting room outside the ICU. Brad wanted to remain at his brother's side, but we encouraged him to lie down and try to get some rest.

"I don't want to leave him, Mom," he said.

"Just for a little while," I replied. "Why not keep me company, maybe take a short nap? You'll need your strength this weekend."

Reluctantly, he nodded.

As much as Bob also needed the rest, he would not leave Brent's side. He pulled his chair close, sat down, and leaned on the side of the bed with his head on his arm, part of him always touching Brent. We hadn't eaten much nor cared to, but I seem to remember trying to find a vending machine to get something, anything, into us. I think we ate some stale cheese and peanut butter crackers with coffee or soda to wash it down. Nothing mattered except Brent, but we knew we couldn't function on empty stomachs forever.

Brad and I asked the nurses at the ICU station for a couple of blankets, and went out to the waiting room to try to get as much sleep we could. He lay down on one of the couches, and I took the recliner chair, but neither of us slept well. We wanted to keep checking on Brent, but that wasn't easy. We had to be admitted through the security door to get back into the ICU. After a while, I heard Brad breathing deeply, and so I did go in to check on Brent. I felt torn between spending time with Brent and not wanting Brad to wake up alone in the waiting room. I also wanted to relieve Bob so that he could go lie down. But Bob was more comfortable staying with Brent. He couldn't bear to leave, even for a short time.

It was painful watching Bob, nearly as painful as thinking about Brent. He was visibly crushed. He seemed diminished, shorter than usual; his shoulders slumping, dark circles under his eyes. His skin color had a grayish tinge to it. He was the illustration of the word "grief-stricken." But he was more than sad and disappointed. He was absolutely devastated.

Bob was a good father and loved both his sons. I could see how severely this was affecting him. When Bob wouldn't take a break, I stayed for a while, holding Brent's hand and talking to him then went out to check on Brad. The night went slowly; all of us unsuccessfully trying to grab a bit of fitful rest, praying to God for a miracle.

By early morning, Brad and I gave up trying to get any more rest. In the vending machine down the hall, I found some coffee for Bob and me and a can of Coke for Brad. As the sun rose, we sat with Brent as a family, talking about him and to him. Then Laura and her parents came back into the room. Laura seemed only slightly rested, her eyes red and puffy, obviously struggling.

The neurosurgeon we'd requested came in before he started his rounds and invited us to join him in another room to review Brent's X-rays and test results. Laura decided to stay with Brent while Bob, Brad, and I went with the doctor. She couldn't bear to hear the gory details, and I didn't blame her, but I needed to know everything. I'm not even sure why; perhaps I still hoped that there was some remote possibility we'd find something to question.

The neurosurgeon, of medium height and build, had dark hair, and a kind face. He seemed more genuinely compassionate than the other doctor had been. He went over the events of the day before, the details of the accident, how Brent was brought into the trauma center, the tests they ran, and their reason for determining such a bleak prognosis. He showed us the scans and X-rays of Brent's head and full body. Even to our untrained eyes, the severity of the brain trauma was evident; the right side where he'd landed was badly swollen and compressing the left side.

At the trauma center, Brent had undergone several tests: head and body scans. Both a neurologist and neurosurgeon examined him and declared him brain-dead. Brent could not breathe on his own, move, or respond in any way. The neurosurgeon told us that the tremendous impact of landing on cement caused a trauma, which made his brain swell and stopped any flow of oxygen to his brain stem, the source of communication to his body. He had no brain activity. The doctor told us that the brain, which controls all functions, cannot regenerate cells and heal itself. Nothing could be done.

We studied and restudied the scans and X-rays,

questioned, and prodded the neurosurgeon, but he never wavered from his assessment. Another neurologist and the one from the night before also stopped in during this discussion and reconfirmed the details. The team agreed that the impact was so great; even if he had been wearing a helmet, it would not have made much difference. The doctors told us that if Brent had survived, he would be paralyzed and seriously impaired from the brain damage he had sustained. They questioned whether he would want to live the rest of his life that way. We knew he wouldn't and reluctantly acknowledged that the situation was hopeless. We were crushed all over again.

Sadly, we returned to Brent's room. We sat and stared at him for some time, until as if on cue, the hospital chaplain from the night before came in, asking if we'd reconsider our decision. Or perhaps would we consider at least donating "just" his eyes, skin, and tissues, if not his organs?

I felt myself bristle. Her request was unfathomable to me. I wanted to shoot her! Skin? How would they even harvest it, peel it? That thought was so repulsive, I couldn't even consider it. But I was too sad and too tired to fight or remind her of our reasons. "No!" I said emphatically. "Just leave us alone!"

After she left, I took a few minutes to call my family, and Bob did the same. They in turn would call other family members and friends with the news. Brad called his girlfriend, Krystal, who said she would let his friends know what was happening. In this way, we were able to rely on a loving chain of concerned friends and family, allowing us to be fully present with Brent in these final, difficult moments.

One of the most important calls I made was to thank

and update our friend Kimm who had helped Bob and Brad make the emergency arrangements to fly out to Arizona. Kimm was in the process of mobilizing many of our friends, whose emotional and logistical support would be critical when we returned from Phoenix.

Shortly after the hospital chaplain left Brent's room, and she left abruptly, a priest from a local parish knocked quietly on the doorframe and asked if he could come in. We stood up and greeted him. He was notified by the hospital of Brent's condition and that we'd listed our religion as Catholic.

As he prepared to administer Last Rites, he asked us which sacraments Brent had received thus far, and I told him that Brent had been Baptized, and received First Holy Communion, but had rejected Confirmation as a teenager. I was grateful that the priest offered to confirm him then. Even though we were no longer practicing Catholics, I wanted to cover all the bases for Brent. Our family surrounded Brent's bed while the priest administered both sacraments, expressed his sympathy, and departed.

We understood that we had little time left with our son, but we believed that his spirit was with us in the room, that he somehow knew we were with him and could feel our love.

It was nearing midday and my sister Pat, Brent's Godmother, would be arriving soon. When I reached her by phone the day before, she and her family had been driving from Boston to the Washington DC area to help her youngest daughter move there. Pat arranged to catch the first available flight to Arizona the next morning.

Soon after she arrived, we'd have to take Brent off life support. I could hardly bear to think about it. We needed to tell Brent that it was OK to go, to tell him one last time how much we loved him, and say our good-byes. All I wanted to do was ask him to fight harder for his life.

I thought about how he loved sports and tried most of them. He also loved the structure and discipline of the military. He combined these interests with a wide range of creative pursuits—theater, writing, drawing and even playing a musical instrument. After having had such athletic and creative ability, I realized that Brent would hate being forced to live with such severe physical and mental handicaps as he'd likely have to face.

I flashed back to the art classes we'd taken together and the pride I felt seeing his drawings, reading his stories, or watching him play sports or perform onstage. I felt grateful to have shared it with him.

Brent was always vibrant and in control. At fifteen, he'd talked us into letting him move out to attend a military high school in New York. We had to spend his college money on it and he agreed to help us pay for college.

Brent seemed to know what was best for him. We knew he was bright, and he went from flunking science and generally underachieving as a freshman at the local public high school to becoming an accomplished student and led the cadet population at New York Military Academy. He earned the position of Third Captain, Chief of Staff, leading the cadet population. Brent was captain or co-captain of at least three sports teams; he achieved academic and athletic awards and earned a full scholarship to Arizona State University, his top choice college. I felt like we had gone from pushing a wet noodle uphill to barely being able to keep up with him as he pursued his dreams.

Despite the high standards for admission, Brent was

striving to join the army aviation program, his goal to be an Apache or Comanche jet helicopter pilot. He'd already passed his written aviation exam and was prepared to pass his physical exam when the accident happened. As we stood there in his hospital room, I thought, *Brent, you were motivated, always thinking ahead. Why couldn't you have thought far enough ahead to realize that getting on this motorcycle was such a bad idea?*

The waiting room was no longer filled with his friends and family today as it had been the day before. Now it was just us; his immediate family, Laura, and her parents.

When Pat arrived in Brent's room, she hugged all of us, one at a time, and expressed her empathy. Then she went to Brent and kissed him and talked to him as she quietly checked his medical condition. Being a nurse, Pat had a better understanding than we had of the medical details and complications.

When the nurse came in, Pat had more questions for the medical staff, but nothing changed the fact that only a miracle could have saved Brent. We all stayed in the room, not wanting to miss a minute with Brent, but also aware that Pat hadn't spent much time with him. We gave her as much space as she needed by clearing some space around his bed.

We asked about her trip. She told us what a shock my call had been and how she'd decided almost immediately that she needed to fly out to Arizona to say good-bye to Brent. Her husband, Paul, would help their daughter, Kim and granddaughter, Chalee, unload and get their things settled in their new place. Pat said that she'd spent a lot of time crying and praying for Brent on the long flight West and was glad to finally be here.

I watched everyone spend these last moments with Brent. It was deeply and unspeakably sad. We stood, surrounding the head of the bed, touched Brent, kissed him, and talked to him. We were somber, sniffling and holding tissues; I could feel we were all holding back sobs, each of us trying not to set the others off. An ICU nurse would occasionally come in to check on him or see if we needed anything.

In our agony, time seemed to move very slowly, and yet it also seemed to race toward that final moment when we would be letting go of Brent. I wanted Pat to be able to spend a couple hours visiting with him; we planned to take him off life support around 3:00 PM local time. I sensed that was all the time the hospital would allow us. They were getting impatient to free up the bed. We had no choice.

We would remove life support and wait to see if he had the strength and the will to stay alive on his own. I prayed for that miracle. As we got close to three o'clock, we told the nurses that we were as ready as we would ever be.

It was hard watching Brad. He was so shaken by what was happening. His cheeks were colorless with beard stubble forming; his shoulders slumped, and he just kept looking down, like he didn't have the energy or will to lift his head. Every few minutes, he would move close to Brent and touch his hand or foot. Brad was big and strong for his nineteen years, but he didn't look it now. It looked like he'd collapse with little resistance if someone pushed him.

Brad and Brent fought a lot growing up since Brent tended to try to run his younger brother's life for him. Brad was much quieter and had, in many ways, lived in Brent's shadow. The boys seemed to get closer when Brent moved away, first to New York then to Arizona. As they got older and were together for short times at home or when we visited Brent, they got along great. They were both more mature, and they missed each other.

It was obvious that Brad looked up to his older brother. It was not Brad's nature to talk about it much. I'm sure the thought of losing Brent, and becoming an only child, must have been pretty scary. This had to be on a different level for Brad than losing his little brother Robbie, who was stillborn. Brad was only four then, and Brent was there to share his sadness.

I also felt a sense of despair from Laura, but even in this terrible moment, Laura was as beautiful as always. She had long straight blond hair (Brent had always loved blondes), blue eyes, perfect skin, and was in great shape. I remember Brent telling me that the first thing he noticed about Laura was her athletic legs. She was quieter than Brent (most people were), but they complemented each other very well. It was obvious that that they loved each other very much. Laura was different from other girls Brent had dated; she was a couple of years older, intelligent, athletic, creative and self-confident in a quiet way. She was a truly quality person, with good values and a nice family.

Brent and Laura had each been renting separate houses with their own friends but had plans to move in together the following month. Laura had one year left at ASU and would be graduating with a degree in landscape architecture. Brent would have stayed at ASU another year to finish his aviation major and get commissioned as an army officer. As an army pilot, he'd have to commit to eight years of active duty. They'd planned to get married in the month between his college graduation and reporting for active duty so that Laura could come with him as an army wife, when possible. They both loved children and planned to have more than one. I was secretly optimistic since there were twins in both sides of Laura's family. I loved the idea of being a grandmother. All of this was fading before my eyes as we watched Brent hooked to those damn machines. Laura's face was white as she touched Brent, not wanting to let go.

Finally, the nurse came in. "Are you ready?" she asked.

I remember thinking, *How could we be ready for this? Did we have any real choice? Damn it! Wake up, Brent, this is your last chance!*

We told the nurse that we'd each say one last good-bye, and then we'd be ready. We took turns, each trying to say their private good-byes and kissing him on the forehead while the others tried not to watch. But I couldn't take my eyes off him. I wanted to go last, so I moved toward the end of the bed where I could still have my hand on him but allow others to get near his head. Maureen and Larry went first, then Pat, then Laura, then Brad, then Bob, and finally, me. It was so difficult to hear everyone saying good-bye, especially Brad and Bob.

I could feel Brad's loss of his big brother in the pit of my stomach, or was that my loss? Brad was and remains a kind, empathetic young man; he would feel this loss very deeply. He would also feel our pain. He tried not to cry, but there were silent streams of tears rolling down his face. His eyes, usually hazel, bright and lively, were dark, sunken, and wet.

Bob's skin was a sickly reddish-gray color, accented by his beard stubble as he hadn't been able to shave. The dark circles under his eyes had continued to deepen. I could see that he was struggling, fighting to hold on.

I can only imagine what I must have looked like, but I didn't care. When it was my turn, I tried to keep my composure. I did not want to further upset everyone. At the same time, I wanted Brent to know how much I loved him and how much I was going to miss him. How was I going to live without this bright, provocative personality in my life? He kept me on my toes; he was full of surprises. He challenged me and forced me to figure out how to handle so many things—whether to help him get him out of a jam or just love him even when I was mad at him.

Could any of us survive without Brent? Our children are not supposed to die before we do. This must be a terrible dream, a nightmare that I would wake up from, right? But it was real. I held on to him for what seemed like both an eternity and an instant. I held Brent's hand and kissed it, then I held his face in my hands and kissed his forehead, his eyelids, and his nose; then I kissed my fingertips and touched them to his lips. He was my baby. This was the last time I was going to hold him.

The first time I'd held Brent, immediately after his birth, I felt such a strong bond with him, like nothing I'd ever felt before. I knew then what it meant to be a mother, responsible for protecting her child. I suddenly transformed from a person who couldn't hurt anyone, even to save myself, to someone who would have killed anyone who tried to hurt my son. But I couldn't protect him from this.

When the doctor had placed him on my chest, Brent let loose a stream of urine that struck me on the chin, narrowly missing my mouth, and I knew he was going to be a challenge. I remember wondering what his life might be like and how it might change our lives in the midst of our married love and happiness. Very soon, he would have that mischievous glint in his eye that would give us a clue. What a ride this young man would take us on: many emotions, ups, downs, and challenges before his life ended just twenty-one years later.

I stood there, praying that when they disconnected that respirator, he might breathe on his own. Yet I realized this was unlikely. I was still beating myself up wondering how I could let them take him off life support.

I had to let go. I shook my head sadly, hugged and kissed him one last time, and told him it was time to go. I also told Brent to keep an eye on us, especially his brother Brad, and to look for Robbie and his grandparents on the "other side".

I glanced up and heard myself saying out loud, "I love you, Brent." I nodded to the nurse to go ahead. We backed away from his bed to make room for the staff. First, the nurses detached the IV then the monitors. Finally they removed the respirator. The nurses took the tubes out of Brent's nose and blood spurted out. I didn't notice, but later, Brad, who is extraordinarily observant, told me how shocked he was at that.

Pat had told us what we might expect when they disconnected the respirator. There would probably be some muscle contractions as the oxygen left Brent's body. His arms might bend upward, but that didn't mean he was waking up. She also told us that his lips or skin might turn blue from lack of oxygen. Pat, Laura, and I were on the right side of the bed; Bob and Brad were on the left side—all of us touching Brent's chest, face, or arms. Maureen and Larry, Laura's parents, waited just outside the room, not wanting to intrude on such a solemn moment. They watched through the door, sad and worried about their daughter.

The nurse made a quick motion, nodded, and left the room. There it was, he was on his own. I could still feel Brent's heart beating under my hand. I needed to feel his heart as it was beating, and when it stopped beating, to know I was with him at the very end. We all felt that way—all five of us had a hand on his chest. There was barely room, but we shared that, and this moment, just like we shared Brent and our love for him.

I remember noticing that the quiet, steady rhythmic sounds of the monitors and respirator were gone, no more *whoosh* as air was pushed into Brent. His chest stopped rising and falling. Then as Pat had warned us, his forearms moved upward slightly and his body felt taut. Then his lips started to turn blue, a weird grayish, bluish purple framed by the pale pink of the skin around his mouth. We felt his heart slow down, and finally, his heart stopped beating. I wanted to scream, "No!" but instead, I pressed my hand onto his chest and felt nothing . . . nothing, no beat, no movement.

It was over. Brent was gone. I began sobbing, trying to choke back the sound, trying not to make it worse for everyone; but they were doing the same thing. We gave Brent one last squeeze and turned to hug each other. I hugged Laura and told her how sorry I was then hugged Pat and cried, before I went around to Bob and Brad. I broke down again when I hugged Brad. He seemed small, like a young child again, even though he was bigger than me. Brad told me it had been two days of "hoping" for him. He said, "Mom, this was our last chance for a miracle." Brad buried his head in my shoulder and sobbed. Finally,

Bob and I hugged and cried in each other's arms, without words, for a long moment, neither of us believing this was really happening.

Maureen and Larry came back into the room and hugged us all, expressing their condolences. Brent's death affected them deeply as well. We stood around Brent's bed with red swollen eyes, not knowing how to console each other, not wanting to leave.

REFLECTION:

Upon reflection, I now realize I was in <u>denial</u> and <u>bargaining</u> all the way to the end until I felt Brent's heart stop beating under my hand. I needed proof that the situation was hopeless and that we had exhausted all available options. Then I finally entered what would eventually be the <u>acceptance</u> stage as I sat there with his lifeless body.

I feel so much empathy for families whose child is lost or in those cases where there is no body recovered. It must be extremely difficult to <u>accept</u> the reality of the death and allow healing to begin.

Because of the nature of his death, the declaration of his being "brain-dead" before we agreed to end life support, there is still a conflict in my mind about his official date of death. His death certificate says May 31, when they pronounced him brain-dead, but his gravestone and my records say June 1. I got the doctor to agree to change the date, but the hospital or Arizona bureaucracy never executed on it.

For them, it was just paperwork. For us, it felt like they were taking away our last day with him. To others, it may seem like a small point, but it still affects me deeply, even now.

I was really <u>angry</u> during much of this time. <u>Angry</u> at my son for taking that needless chance, <u>angry</u> at the hospital for valuing their procedures over the pain and grief we were obviously experiencing, <u>angry</u> at the motorcycle manufacturer for allowing these "rice rockets" on the roads, maybe even angry at ourselves for not preventing it.

I can only hope that professionals handling these situations remember the "unnatural" tragedy playing out most likely for the first time in each family. Our individual loss and grief turns our world upside down and won't always "fit" within hospital or municipal procedures and protocols. Ideally, over time, there will be training designed to increase sensitivity around families losing a child. I've heard from other parents that some locations are much improved at this now.

Chapter 4

Dealing with What Remains

THE NURSES CHECKED on us but left us alone as we absorbed what had just taken place. With difficulty, Laura and her parents said their final good-byes to Brent and headed home, with our promise to come to their house the next day for dinner; some of their extended family were staying with them. As Bob, Brad, Pat, and I started saying our good-byes to Brent, the nurses came back in and said they needed to prepare his body for the next step.

"What is the next step?" I asked.

"He'll have to go to the medical examiner," the lead nurse said, "for an autopsy." This was shocking news, the first we'd heard that an autopsy would be required! I felt my anger return, thinking of Brent being cut open.

"What? Why the hell would my son need an autopsy?"

They stood there with wide eyes, looking at me like I should have known, somehow.

"Look," I said. "We already decided not to donate organs so we could keep his body intact. I thought that was clear! No one mentioned that an autopsy was part of this process. If we'd known you were going to do an autopsy anyway, we might have decided differently."

The lead nurse just stared at me for a moment then said, "I'm sorry, but this wasn't my decision. It is state policy in the event of an accident." Then she added, "It is standard procedure."

"I don't care about your standard procedure! How can I stop it?" I was nearly shouting now even as I felt a little sorry for the short dark-haired nurse taking the brunt of my wrath.

"Why didn't anyone explain that earlier?" I said.

She made no reply.

I was feeling myself back in tigress mode, fighting for my son even though he was dead. It was important to protect his body, his dignity, and preserve him for his wake and funeral—the last time his family and friends would see him. He would have wanted that.

I realized I wasn't getting anywhere. Calming myself, I began asking specific questions. "What does the state do with the results? Are they running different tests than the trauma center ran? How can I reach the medical examiner and try to dissuade them from an autopsy?"

Sensing my fear, the nurse softened a bit and explained that the state required an autopsy for any accident on a public road, as a matter of policy. It was primarily to determine if there had been substance abuse or negligence as well as assessing if the state had any potential liability.

She checked and confirmed that the trauma center had already run the same tests the medical examiner would run and then some. All required information was already a part of Brent's medical record.

"I would suggest writing a letter to the medical examiner,"

she said, "and we can put the letter and a copy of the medical tests with Brent's body when it goes there, which it must, by law. Then you can try to reach the M.E. by phone." The nurse got me some plain paper to write on.

We moved to the waiting room to let the nursing staff prepare Brent's body. I spent the next half hour writing and revising what I hoped was a compelling plea to avoid the autopsy. Pat and Bob offered their feedback; I made revisions until I had a neat handwritten final letter.

Brad kept going back in to check on Brent. He was understandably finding it so very hard to leave his brother. It was difficult to watch. Bob was being protective of Brad, occasionally checking on him, gently nudging him to let go, telling him Brent was gone and we'd have to leave soon.

When I glanced in briefly while working on the letter, Brent's room looked different somehow. The inside lights were dimmed, and dusk was approaching, giving the room a gray, depressing aura. Brent lay on a pillowless gurney, perfectly flat, very still. Brad stood next to his bed, head down and shoulders slumped, clothes wrinkled, with the shadow of a beard. He was leaning in, whispering softly to his brother, his hand on Brent's pale shoulder. The dim fluorescent light behind the bed caught the sheen of Brad's tearstained face. Painful.

I gave the letter to the nurse and asked them how to reach the medical examiner by phone. She explained that it wasn't easy on the weekend. It was now Saturday, and the medical examiner's office wouldn't work on Brent until Monday, but she gave me the number.

I was on a mission. I called and left messages, talked to assistants, then called back several times, hoping to have someone who had decision-making authority call me back before leaving the hospital. I felt helpless and violated. These people were treating my son like a statistic, a number. Brent had his accident at seven thirty in the morning after passing a test that proved his readiness to take the formal physical fitness test for the army aviation program. I knew there were no substance issues here. Brent was training to serve his country. He had simply overestimated his abilities and underestimated the difficulty in handling his friend's motorcycle. It was a tragic accident.

A medical examiner did call me back, and I explained our situation. I told her that we'd forwarded the tests run upon Brent's admission to the trauma center, along with the letter we wrote; both accompanied his body. I suggested that a review of these tests would yield the information they required. I pleaded with her to waive the autopsy so that we could leave our son's body intact and allow for an open casket with him in uniform. After a short discussion, she conferred with her boss and agreed. I was so relieved that I cried.

I could leave the hospital now, let Brent's body go to the next step, and feel that I had somehow protected him in a way that he'd want. This was very important to me. I thanked the medical examiner profusely, got off the phone and told Bob and Pat. We all breathed a little easier.

A short time later, a hospital nurse came to tell us we could go into Brent's room one last time. Brad was still in there; Bob, Pat, and I entered hesitantly. There was no motion in Brent's chest and no sound from the respirator or monitors, but we did notice another significant difference—the room had gone cold. I could feel that Brent's spirit was gone.

We reminded Brad that his brother was with Robbie and his grandparents now and he'd always be with us in our thoughts, but it was time to go. The nurse informed us that Brent would be picked up shortly. It was hard to leave our son, the room, and the hospital where he died. We did so reluctantly.

Maureen and Larry had made a hotel reservation for us nearby in Scottsdale, gave us directions, and lent us a car to use while in Arizona.

Earlier, I'd asked Pat to call a friend of hers, Hank, who was a mortician back home in Massachusetts. I knew he spent quite a bit of time in Arizona and had contacts in the area. Also, he knew Brent, and we were confident that he would ensure that Brent's body was taken care of respectfully. I called him now, and he offered to arrange for a colleague in the Phoenix area to pick up Brent's body from the medical examiner. Hank told us that the Arizona mortician would need to embalm Brent, a requirement before any commercial airline would fly his body home. Hank would then pick Brent up at the airport and prepare him for the wake and funeral back in Massachusetts. I hated thinking about Brent in the cold dark cargo space of a large jet, but it was the only realistic option other than cremation, which we'd decided against. It was a tremendous relief to have a friend, someone we knew and trusted, take over this difficult and heartbreaking task.

Pat, Bob, Brad, and I were all emotionally and physically exhausted. It was near dinnertime, and we needed some "fuel" even though grief kept us from feeling hungry. We found the car Laura's parents had left for us in the hospital parking lot, put our things in it, and headed to the hotel, only fifteen minutes away. Everything always seemed more spread out in Arizona compared to New England.

I checked us into the hotel, and we gratefully headed to

the average economy room with the two double beds we were sharing. We'd already generated many unanticipated expenses on this trip to Arizona, and we still had more to do before leaving. But right now, we were barely able to walk and talk; we were done for today. We each took turns showering and then walked to the onsite restaurant—one of the Red Lobster franchises. It was Saturday evening, and we did not care what we ate, we just needed something and a drink to help us relax. Of course we felt melancholy; we ate, but I have no recollection of what we had for dinner. We talked about the last two days and reminisced about Brent, each of us in turn occasionally choking back tears. At the end, we were glad to get back to our room and crash. We were all in bed by 9:00 PM.

I believe that night was the first direct contact I had from Brent. Along with being extremely sad, I was still angry at Brent. I recognized that the accident had been a result of his need for adventure, and knew he had talked his friend Oz into letting him drive that motorcycle. I was angry that he'd been so careless, putting Laura and our families through all this.

His spirit must have sensed the anger accompanying my grief. As exhausted as I was and as soundly as I always sleep, I woke up at approximately 3:00 AM and heard Brent's voice saying, "Forgive me." At that point, I wasn't sure what I believed about afterlife, but I knew in my mind and in heart that it was Brent. I clearly sensed that he needed me to forgive him so that his spirit would release and be allowed to move on.

I was sharing one bed with my sister. Bob and Brad were sharing the other one. I was on the side near them with only a couple feet of space between us. When I heard

Brent and sat up, I looked over, and Bob and Brad were awake too. I moved over to sit on their bed, and I told them what I'd heard and felt. We just sat and hugged each other and cried. We woke Pat up in the process, and she didn't know what to do to comfort us. She later told me that she was torn between trying to share this moment with us and allowing us privacy. She cared deeply but felt somewhat awkward, like a "fifth wheel." It was important to me to have her there, but I probably wasn't thinking clearly enough to tell her that at the time.

The real pain and the full realization that Brent was gone were just starting to set in. I didn't know then that it would get much worse before it got any better. We cried until we couldn't cry any longer, like we ran out of tears. I got back on the other bed, and we all settled down and tried again to sleep.

Though fitful, we finally did get some rest. Pat got up for an early flight and said she'd get breakfast at the airport. Laura's uncle had offered to bring her there. Paul was driving home from Virginia and would pick her up in Boston. Their daughters, Stacey in South Carolina and Kim, now in Virginia, would follow in a few days. Pat hated to leave us but wanted to get back to her family and console them. Her entire family had been very close to Brent, and it would be hard on all of them. We hugged good-bye, thankful she had a ride to the airport—one less thing to deal with.

We tried to fall back asleep again, but it didn't work; so we got up that Sunday morning, dressed, and found a place for breakfast. We had more painful work to do that day: the task of going through Brent's belongings. With the help of Laura's family and the ROTC, we'd decided to hold a local service for Brent in a Catholic chapel on the ASU campus on Monday.

We had a flight home on Tuesday. Brent's body would arrive back in Massachusetts on Wednesday; then Brad's high school graduation was Thursday evening. We had already decided to hold Brent's wake on Friday and his funeral on Saturday. It was a hell of a week facing us. There was so much to do, and we had to keep going. The protective numbness, which shrouded us, helped us to get through it.

After breakfast, we headed over to Chandler, Arizona, where Brent rented a house with two other guys, Tom and Mark and their three dogs: a brindle Great Dane, a Weimaraner, and Brent's dog, a red-nosed Pit Bull named Brutus. It was a pleasant three-bedroom stucco house with a small fenced-in yard in a nice neighborhood. A few of Brent's friends were already there, but just leaving, including Oz. We hadn't seen them since the night of our arrival, which seemed like ages ago. They expressed their condolences and told us what a good guy and great friend Brent had been, how this was such a shock to them. It was apparent that Oz was feeling particularly badly. He still had Brent's car; he'd driven it over and gave us the keys.

Brad took Brent's car for a spin, probably an attempt at being close to his brother. The car, a sporty white Acura 5-speed, would be his now. During the drive, he said he listened to a song called "This Is How You Remind Me" by Nickelback, a song which he and Brent both liked and had listened to together.

I spoke with each of Brent's friends and gave each of them a hug before they left. I told them that I'd love it if they'd give up motorcycle riding, or at least promise me that they would never get on a motorcycle without a helmet. They couldn't refuse me the last part and promised to at least always wear a helmet. I felt only slightly better. I remember wondering why helmet laws weren't in place in all states and whether that would have made a difference.

Now we had to figure out what to do with the things Brent had left behind—starting with his puppy, Brutus. Bob and I had flipped out when he told us he'd gotten a pit bull. Because he'd anticipated our reaction, Brent didn't tell us about the dog until after he'd paid for Brutus, brought him home, and had a veterinary program in place for him. Brent lived across the street from the breeder and had been easily persuaded to buy one of a litter of new puppies. Our son maintained that the problems with pit bulls were a result of how they were or weren't trained, not because of anything inherent in the breed itself. We thought he was crazy. But he took Brutus running daily and worked hard on training him, and the dog turned out to be a sweet, loving pet. He was still not fully grown, just under a year old, when Brent died. We'd met him when we came out for Brent's birthday three weeks earlier, so he remembered us now.

Both Laura and Brutus were at Brent's house when we arrived. Brutus came running to greet us, but he acted a bit strange too. He glanced at us anxiously and then around the room. His anxiety made me wonder if he knew that his owner was not coming back. Animals seem to sense these things, and I think I felt that from him. I sat on the beige rug with him, feeling his soft warm coat, hugged him and cried. He, Laura, and memories were all I had left of Brent, along with his few possessions. This was all still sinking in, it still didn't feel real.

We knew we had a decision to make about Brutus because he was family now. Back home, we had a miniature schnauzer named Gizmo, Brent and Brad's first dog. We were certain she'd be a nervous wreck with Brutus around. We also knew that East Coast culture was far less supportive of pit bulls. Some states had passed laws requiring special insurance if you had them living in your house. But Brutus was so special to Brent; we couldn't just get rid of him.

Then Laura came to the rescue and asked if she could keep Brutus. She said that Brent had recently asked her to take care of him if anything ever happened to him. We thought it odd that Brent would make a request like that so recently but wanted to comply with his wishes, and we were grateful that problem was solved. Brutus was now Laura's. Brad would have taken him home in a heartbeat, but he understood it was best for Brutus and all of us that he remain with Laura. She also seemed to need to keep that connection to Brent.

I held Brutus as he squirmed for a few minutes, and then I pulled back and looked him in the eyes. He was a beautiful golden color, and his eyes were the same color as his fur. Those eyes seemed to say so much; there was so much unconditional love there. I imagined the questions in those eyes: "What is going on? What is different today? Where is Brent?" He looked right back at me for a few seconds then started to lick my face, almost like he was trying to console me. I hugged Brutus tightly again and thought of him being the closest thing I had to a grandchild.

The common area of the house was neat for having three guys and three dogs living there. It had a cathedral ceiling with skylights. A counter separated the open kitchen and living room, and sliding glass doors led to a fenced-in backyard. Brent's room was off a short hallway from the living room along with two other bedrooms and a bathroom. That was messier and more crowded than the common area with an unmade queen-size bed, a dresser, a stack of books, and various posters on the walls.

Time to start the work we dreaded. This was so hard, about the most difficult thing I could imagine. How could we be disposing of our son's things? It was like disposing a part of him. Wouldn't he need them? Wasn't this a bad dream? Wasn't he going to show up any minute with that big grin and cocky attitude and say, "Hey, what are you guys doing with my stuff?"

We started with the closet. We found his dress greens, his formal army uniform. We knew that was what he'd want to be buried in; it had to come home with us. We stood there caressing it for a few minutes, trying to choke back emotion. Every time we picked something up of his, we had to touch it, smell it, and remember the last time we saw him wearing it. This was a slow and painful process.

His army T-shirts made me think of his running six miles every morning before the Arizona heat got too bad. His camouflage pants and heavy boots reminded me of the stories he told us of long weekend hikes in the desert with full gear and thirty-five-pound backpacks complete with stories of shaking snakes and tarantulas out of his sleeping bag. As I'd pick up a piece of clothing I'd bought for his birthday or that he'd worn on one our trips or adventures together, those memories would come flooding back. Sometimes, I'd have to take a break and give Brutus a hug. He was the closest I could get to Brent.

Clothes were on the floor that should have been hanging up. There were piles of clean underwear on his dresser and T-shirts stuffed in the drawers. We began to separate what we might take with us, like his T-shirts, sweat pants, and jackets. We wanted Brad to take whatever he wanted, but he was still too dazed to decide. As a teenager, he'd already outgrown Brent in height as well as clothes and shoe sizes, so most of Brent's things would not fit him. Some would fit Bob. We all wanted something of his we could touch, wear, or be close to. Anything—even if it didn't fit. We knew our extended family would too.

Brent's roommate, Tom, was a similar size and weight to Brent and had the same shoe size. We started making two piles, one to bring home and one for Tom, Mark and Brent's friends to look through. Laura and Brad got first choice. Brad chose a Boston Patriot's football team flask with Brent's initials, BRD, the same as his. He also took Brent's army baseball cap and some golf items, not much else.

We gave Brent's shoes, army boots, and two pair of expensive roller blades to Tom. We hated to throw anything away. It felt somehow like we'd be throwing a piece of Brent away. Given a choice, we would not have dealt with his belongings so soon, but we had to take care of his affairs before our flight home. We also understood his roommates would need his stuff cleared out so they could get someone to take over Brent's share of the rent. I hoped he'd already paid for that month that was just beginning, though I'm not sure we even thought to ask. We were functioning like zombies, mechanically—not full function.

In the living room, Laura and friends were putting together a photo collage for his memorial service. Laura was so creative, and she really wanted to have some of the pictures she'd gathered from their life together as part of a tribute to Brent.

Since his Arizona memorial service was set for the next day, we needed to finish going through Brent's things both at his apartment and at Laura's house. Monday morning, we still had to go to the bank and close his accounts, see the accident site, attend his service Monday afternoon, and be ready to depart Tuesday morning.

Brent's commanding officer, Colonel Crawford, offered to take the lead in arranging a service for Brent on campus. We gratefully accepted his offer, and Laura's family volunteered too. They were all wonderful, very helpful, and understanding. The colonel, an army officer and leader of these young men, was a parent with a family of his own. He made it as easy as he could on us. I got the feeling that he was very empathetic and felt partly responsible because this happened on his "watch." He was getting ready to transfer to a new assignment in another state, but he made sure that he had a backup leader who was involved and informed should we have ongoing needs.

Laura's parents and her family planned flowers and food for the ceremony and a gathering after. We were so grateful. Brent's ROTC buddies also assisted in planning the ceremony at the Catholic chapel on campus, which seemed fitting and appropriate. The task that remained for us was to get an obituary into the local paper. I couldn't even manage that on time and missed the paper's deadline midday on Monday.

Because Brent's body was being embalmed, it was not to be at the Monday service. I had no idea what other details were being taken care of by others. When anyone needed a decision, they'd call and ask me, and I'd answer in a sort of a fog and trust they'd handle it somehow. Looking back, things weren't fully registering, I couldn't be my usual control-freak self.

Back in Brent's room, we finally finished sorting through

Brent's stuff and had a huge pile for his friends to go through. We also had two of his green army duffel bags full of clothes for us to bring home and another pile to go in the trash. Laura had taken a few things that were important to her, like his baseball cap or a T-shirt she knew he loved and she could wear to bed.

We took a much-needed break, got cold drinks, and sat in the living room with Laura and Brent's roommates, talking about him, and looking at the photo collage they'd put together. The pictures prompted us to tell stories about Brent and laugh about him, but the chuckle would sometimes turn into tears. We decided to wrap up our visit and head to Laura's house in Tempe. It wasn't easy to leave. This was the last time we'd be at Brent's home in Arizona.

We'd been to Laura's before, a lovely house that also had three bedrooms not far off the ASU campus. Laura had a pool table where she and Brent had shot countless games. Bob and I had played with them when we visited—boys against girls. Brent would get very focused if it looked to him like Laura and I were catching up and might beat him. He'd become even more competitive. Now it was painful to pull up to Laura's house and the familiar surroundings that Brent had loved— with thoughts about his not returning there . . . or anywhere.

Brent didn't have as many things here as he'd had at his house, but there was still a lot. It was just as painful, maybe even more so because they shared this space together as a couple. When Bob, Brad, and I had come out to Arizona May 8th for Brent's birthday, we'd taken them to dinner in Phoenix at the French restaurant where he'd just gotten a part-time job so he could save for an engagement ring.

During that lovely Wednesday evening dinner, they'd told us they were moving in together. They'd found an apartment to share and were signing a lease the next week with a plan to move in July. We knew this relationship was serious, and since we also loved Laura, we were very happy for them. Still, it was a big step. They were beaming, and we congratulated them, ordered champagne, and toasted them. We were so happy and asked the waiter to take a picture of the five of us at the table. Now the memory of that conversation and that weekend haunted me as we helped Laura go through Brent's things.

That weekend had been our last together with Brent; we'd taken him to Las Vegas for his twenty-first birthday. Bob and Brad flew out early and took Brent golfing that day, one of his favorite things. I flew out later that day after a mandatory business meeting, and they picked me up at the airport to head to dinner together. I remember Brent standing out in front of the others in the area just beyond security, grinning, waiting to greet me. He looked fit, tan, and handsome. I was so proud of him and couldn't wait to give him a big birthday hug.

I ran to him, yelling, "Happy Birthday!" I hugged him hard, gave him a big kiss on the cheek. After all, my eldest son was officially an adult now; not that he could do anything more adult than he was already doing, but it hit me that he was all grown-up! At the restaurant, he introduced us to everyone where he now worked; he seemed so proud to have his family there. He chose the wines and recommended food, and I remember wondering, *Is this* my *son?* The one who often got in minor trouble in school and struggled with freshman science? He seemed so worldly, so confident, so in control, and at ease. It was awesome to see. The five of us had a wonderful dinner. Laura was already part of the family, a lovely addition.

We'd been forced to cancel our trip several times because of my demanding work schedule, but I was determined to get us out there for Brent's big day. Then we took the family, including Laura, to Las Vegas for the weekend to celebrate. I can't begin to describe how grateful I am that we got to spend that weekend with Brent just three weeks before his accident. We hadn't seen him since Christmas, and it would have been hard to forgive myself if I hadn't made the trip happen.

The four of us flew to Vegas the next morning, Thursday. Laura had an event to attend in Phoenix and joined us early Saturday morning. We had a long weekend doing fun things in Las Vegas seeing the casinos, going on the rides, doing a little gambling (Brent won), seeing a show, and eating in unusual restaurants. We even found a place for Brad to get his first tattoo, although his father was upset at him for doing that and at me for helping him. Brad was nineteen. I knew he was going to do it anyway, and I just wanted to make sure he got his tattoo in a safe clean place. The odd thing was that Brent played peacemaker that evening between Bob and me, an unusual role for him in the family. While I'd heard he did that sort of thing often as a leader with his high school cadet population, I hadn't seen him in action. We were having such a fun weekend, and I think Brent just wanted to make sure none of us ruined it; little did we know it was our last weekend together.

Laura showed up in time to join us for breakfast Saturday morning. We walked through some of the more elegant casinos together. We went to see the fountains, Chihuly glass and botanical gardens in the Bellagio, the Italian tile and gondolas at the Venetian, and more. Laura, loved that sort of thing. As always, Brent lit up when Laura was in the room; they were so in love. We went to Emeril's restaurant for dinner. Then, because Laura loved the movie *Coyote Ugly*, I took them over to the bar of that name in the New York-New York casino, paid their way in, bought their first drink, then left them alone to have some fun on their own (after I had a drink poured into my mouth by the waitress standing on the bar, of course—their signature gesture).

We all met a little later, did some gambling, and finally got some sleep. We had breakfast in a new place Sunday and did some more exploring that morning. Then we put Brent and Laura on a shuttle bus to the airport in front of the MGM Grand, where we stayed, midday Sunday. They were catching the short return flight to Phoenix; they had classes the next day. We gave them a big hug and kiss before they got on the bus, told them to stay in touch, that we loved them, and would we'd see them soon. I'm sure we gave Brent some sort of advice too, and a little extra cash; it was sort of a ritual. I hated to see Brent and Laura leaving; they were so much fun to be with. I felt very blessed just then with my wonderful expanding family.

I'm not sure that we'd have done anything differently if we had known that it was the last time we'd see Brent alive. It was clear to us that he knew we loved him and were proud of him. That was very important, and I felt very fortunate not to have many regrets later on. Brent and I had had our share of fights, but we always made up afterward. We'd been able to take several trips as a family, and I especially treasured the mother-son trips I'd taken with the boys, individually or together. We had many special moments on those trips.

Just then, Brutus came up and licked my hand, bringing me out of my daydreaming. My mind snapped back to the present task at hand in Laura's house in Tempe that Sunday afternoon. She was going through closets and drawers, pulling out Brent's things, the pain visible on her face. There were some clothes and CDs and DVDs. She offered them to Brad; he took a couple and left the others for her. Thankfully, there were fewer of Brent's things there, but it was every bit as painful, especially for Laura. It would be hard for her to go on living here without him, so she planned on staying with her parents in Phoenix while she figured things out.

We had been invited to dinner at Maureen and Larry's home—our family, Laura's aunt, and a couple of friends. It was low key and friendly. They wouldn't let us do or bring anything. They just wanted to take care of us. We were more like extended family than in-laws. I was hoping that would continue. Laura's mother and I were already good friends. Maureen was a friendly, warm, and caring person. Laura's Dad, Larry, was quieter but just as nice, very creative, and an excellent cook. I could see where Laura got her warm personality, intelligence, and creativity. We had a relaxing dinner and told stories about Brent, which was very healing. We even got to laugh a little, something we hadn't done in what seemed like a long time. It was a good release. We left reasonably early, exhausted from an emotional day. While the work was not hard physically, it was the hardest work I'd ever done.

Still using the borrowed car, we drove back to the hotel and crashed, this time with Bob and me in one bed and Brad in the other. How many times had we traveled and Brad shared that other bed with Brent? I'd taken countless pictures of them sleeping together when they were young, on their knees, with their little butts in the air, so cute in their cartoon character underwear. I'm guessing that as Brad tried to fall asleep that night, he also thought about never again sharing a bed with his brother.

REFLECTION:

There was so much pain during this time. It's difficult even now to write about. I remember <u>anger</u> and shock at the sudden request for an autopsy and the general lack of communication between the medical caregivers in the hospital. It seemed like everyone was in their own cocoon, insensitive to the fact that this death, this loss, was an extreme and traumatic situation for us, like it would be for any family.

Because we'd been with Brent when his heart stopped beating, to some extent, we had begun the process of <u>acceptance</u>. His actual death could no longer be denied. Yet we had no idea yet what full <u>acceptance</u> would mean to each of us. We would discover that over time—a long time.

<u>Bargaining</u> for Brent's life was replaced by our prayers for help and strength to get through this awful process. Numbness set in early for protection and to help us through the necessary steps of dealing with the funeral-related tasks.

But what do we do with our child's things? I think it's comforting for close family and friends to have a memento of the loved one that they can cherish. Many parents can't or don't have to deal with their child's belongings right away. It may be a personal decision or a forced situation, like in our case. The temptation may be to treat the child's room or belongings like a shrine indefinitely. I believe our children are okay with us trying to move on, that it helps them too as their spirits continue on.

A child's death is so unnatural and often unexpected. It affects family and extended family, friends, neighbors, teachers, colleagues, and even pets—sometimes strangers too. Besides all the wonderful support we received from people we knew, we also got cards, letters, and books from others we had never met.

Having to leave Brent's body was one of the hardest things we had to do. We felt like we were somehow abandoning him, and for us, that was terrible. Parents are so programmed to protect their children; it is devastating when you no longer can. Perhaps that explains why we fought so hard to protect his body. It was excruciating to leave the hospital and Arizona without him knowing that we might not be back to visit those who'd become part of Brent's life and now were dear friends.

The level of stress and exhaustion through this entire ordeal was horrendous. I think that applies to any family losing a child—in any circumstance. It's very important to be kind to ourselves and each other and not expect a lot. The death of a child is likely the most difficult thing we'll ever endure. We might need help in recovering from the loss, sometimes, professional or medical help. Ideally, we'd also recognize something very important: that so many people around us want to help us. Let them—we all benefit. However, they often don't know how to help, and we may have to tell them what we need, at any given point. Don't expect them to fully understand; they won't be able to if they haven't been through it.

Chapter 5

Wrapping Up Brent's Life in Arizona

MONDAY MORNING, WE awoke after another restless night knowing we had to finish taking care of Brent's affairs. We also felt compelled to see the accident site even though we knew that would be difficult. We made an appointment with the ASU police officer who was among the first at the scene.

The accident happened in front of the Ross-Blakely ASU Law library and behind the ASU police station.

Bob, Brad, and I met the officer at the police station. He offered his condolences and walked us to the accident site—an ugly part of the campus in comparison to other areas. The police officer explained that Brent had driven the motorcycle out of the student parking lot where the bike stalled at the stop sign, directly across the street from the library, and then he recounted the events of the accident.

The policeman's comments mingled with my own thoughts to the point where it seemed hard to separate them. I could hear the sympathy in his voice. It was difficult surveying the scene of my son's death, but I craved to understand the details. I tried to imagine what Brent felt as it was happening and hoped that he was not in pain. He lay unconscious when they got to him three minutes after the accident. They had to cut a hole in his throat and put in a tube to help him breathe. I imagined the friends who saw it, stopping their cars in the street and running to help him; at least I hoped he wasn't alone.

Then I saw it: the bloodstain on the cement. It was faded like it had been washed, but unmistakably, this was my son's blood. I wanted to faint. I knelt on my knees and put my hands on the now-dry pale reddish brown stain. The police officer quietly apologized, saying they'd tried to bleach it, but a little remained. He told us Brent had not lost a lot of blood, but there had been some. I stayed on my knees, sobbing. Bob and Brad came over and laid their hands on my back, and Bob knelt on one knee to touch the spot. It's hard to describe what it's like to see the place where your child died, to shake off the terrible images conjured up from seeing and touching his bloodstains.

After a few minutes, Bob helped me up and I stood, wiping my eyes on my shirtsleeve. The tissues I'd brought were a wet crumpled mess; they couldn't hold any more tears.

I was so exhausted that I just wanted to lie down there and go to sleep forever, right where Brent's life had ended. Though he sounded very far away, the officer, who was actually only a few feet from us, said, "I'm sorry, ma'am, is there anything I can do?"

I came out of my trance and looked at him through my tears, shaking my head. "No, thank you." That was all I could manage.

Leaning on each other, we walked back across the street

to the police station to view the remains of the motorcycle. It was a large motorcycle: black, gray, and silver—very dangerous looking. It had been totaled. The front end was bent and broken, with metal and glass shards scattered about, but the body of the bike didn't look as bad as I expected. Not bad enough to have caused my son's death. It felt similar to when I saw Brent and his injuries didn't look bad enough to cause his death. I was glad the bike was totaled. No one else could get hurt on this motorcycle. I was sorry for Oz's loss, but I didn't want anyone I knew riding motorcycles.

The officer pointed out a few things about the bike, its angles, and how Brent had likely accelerated it. The police tested to see if the accelerator was stuck, in case of equipment malfunction, but it was not. We wanted, I suppose, to think of it as someone else's fault, not just an accident from operator error—in this case, an inexperienced operator.

Out of the corner of my eye, I saw Brad crouching next to the bike, one hand on it, touching it like it was somehow enabling him to touch his brother. His other hand reached for a small piece of the bike that he could keep, something tangible that connected him to his brother's last act or adventure, something that his brother had touched before he died. Brad slipped the small dark gray piece of plastic into his pocket and stood up. He recently told me that he still has it, ten years later. He also told me that at first, he'd blamed Oz. He couldn't understand why he would loan a dangerous motorcycle to anyone; he felt it was like giving a novice a loaded gun. I think Bob felt that way too; I did not.

We thanked the officer, and he shook each of our hands. Then we left slowly, looking back toward the accident site, not really wanting to leave. Brad mentioned that while we were at Brent's house, he overheard one of Brent's friends say that he heard the bike suddenly revving, and it probably kicked into gear by accident. The motorcycle had a fast acceleration feature—zero to sixty in 2.6 seconds—and the distance to the loading dock wall was too short. I thought, if only I could have been there to hold Brent's head in my lap or comfort him in some way. I wondered if any of his angels or relatives that had passed on had been there looking after him; I hoped so. Over and over again, I wondered if he'd felt any pain, how much fear had he experienced in those last moments as he catapulted through the air and hit the cement. I shook my head slowly and got back into our borrowed car.

It was late morning, and we headed over to the bank where Brent had his checking account. We'd found a bank statement at his house the day before and learned that the account contained most of the latest monthly transfer money we'd sent him. On the way there, I thought about his financial and academic situation while at ASU.

Brent had worked hard and gotten a full army ROTC scholarship that covered his tuition and offered some help with living costs, but not enough to completely cover his rent, books, and living expenses. We agreed to send him money every month but suggested he work part-time if he needed or wanted more than that, as long as his grades didn't suffer. Brent had more expensive tastes than we were willing to fund, so he'd gotten a part-time job during college.

It wasn't easy for him; he chose a mechanical engineering major, thinking he should have a backup in case he didn't get into the army aviation program—which did not require a specific major. ASU freshmen with engineering majors lived and took classes together as a group as it was a very challenging curriculum. He did very well in most of his subjects, but calculus gave him problems. He switched his major to computer science for one semester in his sophomore year, but he hated it.

At that point, Bob and I asked him why he was messing around with other majors if his dream was to be an aviator; it was the reason he went the military path. As an aviation major, half his classes would be on the East campus, not the one in Tempe, more than a thirty-minute drive. We didn't allow Brent to have a car on campus his freshman year but agreed he could have my car starting his sophomore year when he'd gotten the scholarship and if he did well his freshman year.

Brent reminded me, came for my car the summer before his sophomore year, and drove it back to Arizona with Laura; so now he had a way to split his classes across campuses. Brent rented the house in Chandler, in between the two ASU campuses, switched his major, and became even more serious about aviation. However, he decided to wait for army flight training, which he felt was more effective than ASU flight lessons. During his junior year, he passed the written test for the army aviation program and was well prepared to pass the physical exam.

My thoughts switched back to the present as we entered the bank and asked to speak to one of the managers. We explained that our son had died. We were only in town for that day and wanted to close his accounts. She asked for his information and our IDs; it was emotional pulling out Brent's ID and closing down even this small part of his life.

We signed some papers, promised to send her a

death certificate, and left with Brent's meager funds. We told Brad we'd put it in his account when we got home; his brother would want that. The bank employee was sympathetic but clearly uncomfortable—our first exposure to how uncomfortable others would be around us when they learned of our bereavement. We finished around lunchtime but weren't very hungry. The last thing on the schedule for that day was Brent's memorial. We had time, so Bob, Brad, and I went back to the hotel.

We hadn't done much physically, but we were exhausted emotionally. Since we had a couple of hours, we tried to relax at the hotel pool. Brad and I bought cheap bathing suits at a local chain store, changed in our hotel room, and the three of us went to the pool. I got a glass of wine at the hotel bar and got Brad a beer. I figured he could use one and was close to legal age. Bob just wanted a soda, so he got one out of the vending machine at the pool. Brad and I stepped into the water while Bob put his coins into the soda machine. As he was walking away, several seconds later, he heard another *clunk*. Bob glanced over his shoulder and saw that a second soda can dropped, on its own. He's not normally given to this kind of thinking, but he was surprised, called to us, wondering if it might have been a little sign or gift from Brent. Maybe it was. We were all grasping for anything that might be a sign.

Brad and I were already over our heads in the pool, both being water rats. We swam a bit, floated, and relaxed then after a while gravitated toward each other then swam to Bob, who was sitting on the pool deck with his bare feet hanging in the water at the deep end.

We talked about Brent, what we were feeling, and how much we'd miss of his life. I spoke of my sense of loss for his children, the grandchildren we'd never have. He and Laura were crazy about kids. Brent had always been wonderful with nearly all of them, except his little brother. I think Brad sensed my loss. "Don't worry, Mom," he said. "I'll have enough kids to make up for Brent." I was moved and felt so close to him at that moment.

"Brad, honey, I love you," I said. "But that is not your responsibility. You need to live your life in your own way."

I assured him that he didn't need to carry the additional burden of trying to live up to what his brother might have done. No one expected that; he was his own person, and we loved him for who he was.

We reminded him that none of us could replace Brent. We made it clear that we appreciated his being so sensitive to the loss we were all feeling. I got off my float and hugged him, and then treading water in the deep end, we both broke down. Bob set his soda can down and reached out to touch both of us. Brad also talked about how he often thought about what Laura must be feeling and how hard it must be for her.

Brent's memorial service was going to be tough, but we would get through it together, as a family.

It was getting late, so we climbed out of the pool, finished our drinks, dried off, and went back to the room to shower and dress for Brent's service. It was still hard to fathom. I hadn't brought enough clothes on the business trip for all the additional time and the range of events. I'd worn the same thing on the flight and all weekend in the hospital, so we'd purchased a few basic things to get through the extra days: black sandals, shorts, slacks, and a blouse—nothing too expensive.

Barely functioning, we didn't care much about how

we looked but agreed it wasn't right to wear jeans to his service. We bought only enough to get by, mindful of the extra costs, but that was unimportant just now. It was something we would have to sort out later.

Maureen and Larry picked us up and drove us to the Catholic chapel on campus where they and the ROTC folks had arranged the service. I was amazed by the young priest, Father Dominic, who greeted us. He was in his twenties, and I remember thinking that you don't see many younger priests these days. He had the most shockingly blue eyes I'd ever seen, one of the warmest smiles—and spiked hair! I couldn't help but smile. He didn't look like any of the priests I had known growing up. Father D offered his condolences and asked us to sit in a room downstairs until they were ready. He asked a few questions about Brent. We felt that he really cared, which was comforting. We had been there only a few minutes when he came back to get us. He escorted me, taking my arm as we came up through the chapel's entry foyer.

What I saw left me overcome with emotion. The chapel was filled with people, the altar full of lovely flowers. A large portrait of Brent on an easel had been set up to the right of the center aisle as we entered. It had been taken recently by Laura; he looked so happy. I felt his presence there with us.

Then I was struck by the crucifix above the altar, so unlike anything I'd ever seen in the many Catholic churches I'd been in. It was a simple wooden cross with an image of Christ's body nailed to it, but it had an abstract, transparent green glass shadow of the body of Christ veering off to the side at an angle. In all my years of visiting churches and attending parochial elementary school, I'd never seen anything like it. This was a young person's chapel on a young person's modern campus. Brent would have liked it. And he would have liked Father Dominic, who was probably not much older than he was.

This caring young priest guided me to a position between Bob and Brad. We three, arms linked, walked down the center aisle to our reserved seats in the first pew on the right. As we passed it, I could not take my eyes off that beautiful sepia-toned picture of my son, which Laura had enlarged and printed.

The image had been taken during a special weekend together at the Camelback resort in Phoenix—not a place they would have been able to afford, but Laura had gotten a good off-season deal for his twenty-first birthday. She'd snapped this endearing photo of him, relaxed and smiling, wearing the silver necklace we'd bought him during his only trip to St. Thomas. We'd ended up buying a time-share during that vacation, intending to will it to him and Brad. The picture captured his good looks and his confident, friendly personality. It felt even more like he was really here with us. On the other side of the center aisle was a second easel with a photo collage of Brent's life in Arizona with Laura, her family, and many of their friends.

We were overwhelmed to see so many of Brent's friends and Laura's family there—more than one hundred people—even though we hadn't gotten the obituary into the newspaper in time. I was touched at this outpouring of caring for Brent.

Sitting between Bob and Brad in the pew comforted me. Brent's commander, officers, and fellow cadet students were present in their army uniforms, looking handsome and patriotic. Two of them moved Brent's portrait from the back up to the side of the altar. I noticed a display at the altar's front and center composed of an American flag, army boots, a rifle, a helmet, and dog tags. Bob explained that it symbolized the "fallen soldier," a memorial tribute that made my eyes fill.

The funeral service started as the young priest in full white vestments with gold trim, and the altar boys in white and black, moving in procession down the center aisle, up to the altar. One of them was carrying a crucifix. It was a lovely service, not a full Mass. Laura, Brent's roommate Tom, and a few other ROTC buddies gave readings, and the priest offered a sermon sharing what he knew of this young man whose life had been cut short. Instead of a eulogy, they did something that meant a great deal to us. Brent's commanding officer and several of his friends got up and shared stories about Brent and how they felt about him; it was wonderful. Some of Brent's friends talked about how adventurous he was—taking risks—or how competitive he was. They told amusing stories about Brent making them play sports or video games over and over until he won at least once. But they also spoke about what a good friend he was, how he was there when anyone needed him, and how he helped the new cadets. It was clear that they felt Brent's passion for life. I knew immediately that we would make this concept a part of his service when we returned home.

We were emotional, yet it was wonderful to hear how much they thought of our son; through their words, we got to know another side of Brent. They invited us to speak, and so the three of us walked up to the pulpit together, holding hands. I spoke first, with Bob and Brad standing behind me. I talked about how proud I was of Brent and all he'd accomplished in his short life, how grateful I was for his friends, Laura, her family, and his ROTC family. I told them I knew he would never have moved back East permanently, because he had grown to love Arizona. I acknowledged how much we'd all miss him and thanked them for supporting him and us.

Bob spoke briefly about what a tragic loss it was and how grateful he was for Brent's support system. Although he was more comfortable when he could prepare his comments, I knew he appreciated the opportunity to speak. When asked, Brad declined to speak. Naturally shy, he just shook his head, keeping his eyes down. He stood behind us, hands clasped, and eyes filled with tears, standing close enough to touch the one of us who wasn't speaking. This was a serious struggle for him because he hated being up in front of people, especially now. When we finished, the three of us nodded thanks and went back to our seat, holding hands.

There was no casket in the aisle, as Brent's body was being prepared to fly home, only his picture on that easel. The priest did a ceremonial blessing around the picture, the fallen soldier display, and finally over us. It was very touching. The ROTC commander gave us a folded American flag housed in a beautiful triangular wood and glass standing case that had a small brass plaque engraved for Brent, another patriotic tribute to him—comforting and something we would treasure.

Father Dominic closed the ceremony with a final blessing for Brent and welcomed the family and guests to a luncheon at the parish hall next door that had been arranged by the ROTC and Laura's family. He and the altar boys recessed with the portable crucifix, formally ending the service. We followed.

I was still fascinated with the abstract crucifix hanging over the altar, I kept looking back at it—so unusual, and somehow it felt so very appropriate.

We walked to the lovely parish hall courtyard next door where Brent's friends and Arizona family had set up tables covered with lovely white tablecloths, rose-filled vases, and an abundance of delicious food. The French restaurant where Brent had only worked a short time contributed to the meal. We filled our plates and picked at them while we talked with Brent's friends and thanked them again. We had a nice talk with both the current and incoming commanding officers. They were complimentary of Brent and offered to help us in any way they could, even after we'd left Arizona.

We really understood what Brent loved about being part of this program; it truly had been a home away from home for him. They'd pushed him to set goals, accomplish them, and feel good about himself while they provided support. He had been wise to join this program. Before we left, as a small token, we donated Brent's TV to the ROTC lounge. We also agreed that we'd use any funeral donations to set up a scholarship fund to help Brent's fellow ROTC students, and started it with our own donation.

It had been a lovely service, luncheon, and celebration of Brent's life; and it was wonderful to meet so many of Brent's friends. I felt sure that Brent was there with us through the entire thing. I could still feel his presence. After the luncheon, Maureen and Larry drove us to our hotel, and their family met us in the lobby to sit and talk over drinks.

It sounds like an odd thing to say, but our last evening in Arizona was wonderful. It had been a chance to get to know Brent's close friends and the family he would have married into. What a waste—such perfect in-laws. We vowed to remain friends and stay in touch; we all got along so well. Laura and her parents were planning to come to Brent's funeral in Massachusetts and would stay with us. We'd see them again soon.

Back at the hotel, we rearranged the comfortable lounge chairs in the lobby bar into a big circle so we could all have a drink and talk. No one was ready to part after such an emotional service. Included in this gathering were Bob, Brad, and myself, Laura and her parents, Maureen's sister Kathy, and brother Tom and his wife, Brent's roommate Tom, and Laura's good friend Sarah and her mother. They felt like extended family to me, and it was obvious they cared about Brent.

As we relaxed and sipped our drinks, the stories started to emerge about Brent and his experiences with them in Arizona. He'd made an impression: friendly, confident, and in love with Laura. Despite not really knowing anyone, he'd gotten up and danced with all the aunts at a family wedding and immediately fit right in. It was easy to recognize our Brent.

Though the day had been hard, I was surprised at how much laughter there was and how comforting it felt. It was much nicer to remember Brent in stories and memories than to wallow in the sadness that enveloped me when I was quiet and thinking too much. I couldn't always keep that sadness at bay, nor was it healthy in the long term to avoid it, but it was great to take a breather, to laugh for a change. It made Brent feel closer talking and laughing about him. He was lucky to have known them; they were nice people and of great comfort to us.

After an hour or so, conversation started to dwindle, and the weight of the situation seemed to set in. We had an early flight, and Maureen's brother offered to take us to the airport, and Larry would pick up the loaner car. There were a lot of hugs and tearful good-byes, expressions of sympathy, and well-wishes from them.

Bob, Brad, and I headed off to our room, absolutely exhausted. We forced ourselves to stay awake long enough to pack so that we didn't have to do it in the morning. Brad stuffed his clothes into his bag and flopped on the bed in his T-shirt and briefs, looking for the TV remote—probably a strategy to avoid talking. Quiet by nature, I was pretty sure he was talked out, struggling with his grief. Bob organized his bag and tossed a few things Brad's way, and I pulled out clothing for the morning, putting everything else back in my suitcase. Bob and I finished and crashed on the other bed. None of us talked much the rest of the evening, just stared silently at the television, not really watching, absorbed in our own thoughts.

I asked myself, "Are we actually going to leave Arizona tomorrow morning, with Brent's body to follow us the next day?" Once we arrived, we needed to prepare for his wake and funeral and somehow get Brad through his high school graduation.

Brent had loved it so much out here. He'd grown up on the East Coast near rivers and the ocean; I never really understood where he got the love of the desert. For him, I knew it was deep and real, almost like he'd lived there in a previous life. The attraction had been instantaneous when we had taken him there on vacation during high school.

I was glad that he had some time to enjoy it; he'd lived in Arizona three years.

Bob, Brad, and I finally fell asleep with the TV on, with the alarm set to wake us up early. At some point during the night, I woke up. The TV was off and the room quiet, but I sensed everyone was sleeping uneasily. The alarm went off at 6:30 AM. I made bad hotel coffee in the room while Bob took a shower. We let Brad sleep a little longer then I showered, and we woke Brad so that we'd be ready to go when Maureen's brother picked us up at 7:30 AM for our 10:00 AM flight.

Phoenix is a huge airport with thousands of people trying to get through security. Since this was less than a year after 9/11, security measures were new and painfully slow to navigate. We were eager to get home, and yet I hated to think about it; there was so much painful work ahead. Thank God we had an army of family and friends waiting to help.

Still, it was hard to leave Phoenix, Brent, and his Arizona family. Because we were bringing Brent's things back with us, we had much more luggage than we'd arrived with. We had both of his duffel bags and his suitcase full, plus we'd packed a large box to be shipped home. We carried anything breakable on board with us as well as the army dress we would bury him in—couldn't take any chances of having that lost.

We said good-bye, thanked Laura's uncle, and literally dragged ourselves through the security and boarding process. I led the way. I'd traveled so much for work that I suspected I could make it through nearly any airport in my sleep, and I wanted to make it as easy as possible for Brad and Bob. Six hours on a plane was bad enough, especially in our state of mind; neither of them was all that fond of flying.

Fortunately, we were able to get a direct flight to Boston, seated together. That way, we wouldn't have to endure someone "chatty" next to us. We faced a very different flight now than the one that had brought us here. On the way out, there was hope; now there was none. All we had to look forward to was Brent's funeral and life without him.

REFLECTION:

Even though we had been with Brent at his passing, visiting the accident scene reinforced our <u>acceptance</u> of what had occurred. Seeing Brent's blood on the cement floor of the loading dock was unbearable. Another dose of reality came as we gave away, discarded, and packed his belongings then closed his bank accounts: we were closing out his life in Arizona. It was impossible to live in <u>denial</u> while going through the painful process of completing these tasks. There was a lot more pain and processing to come; we didn't yet know what to expect. Our fogginess and numbness helped us to function at a minimal level and got us through during this time.

Thank God we had Brad to focus on. I can't imagine what it is like to lose an only child; I can only shudder when thinking of it. After losing a child, bereaved parents become extremely protective of any remaining children, almost smothering. I know Bob and I couldn't help ourselves, at least not at first. In our case, after losing Robbie and Brent, I wanted to put Brad in a protective bubble but understood at the same time that wasn't possible. That was hard. He was nineteen and was out of our sight often. He needed his freedom, of course. I talked to him about it to help him understand that it wasn't that we didn't trust him; it's just that I felt that we needed to protect him, as unrealistic as that was. I didn't know if I'd survive if anything happened to him too although I didn't share that thought with him. I was still <u>bargaining</u>; **only this time it was Brad I was** <u>bargaining</u> **for.**

Even in these early moments, clearly <u>depression</u> *was starting to settle in. We were still essentially numb at this point, profoundly sad, and spinning through so many of the "stages." I've heard that* <u>depression</u> *is "anger turned inward," but I can also recall feeling and expressing* <u>anger</u> *during this time. I felt* <u>anger</u> *at the motorcycle manufacturer for marketing these racing bikes to young men to use on the street,* <u>anger</u> *at God for not complying with my request and giving Brent another chance, and* <u>anger</u> *at having to endure this.*

Even at the beginning, we knew we had support from family and friends; that made a huge difference. They felt like our safety net; I could literally feel them at my back, holding me up. It must be indescribably difficult for families to go through this alone or without that kind of support. I can only hope that I can help others in some small way, through my work with bereaved families.

We need someone to listen to us, to hug us, to help us with menial tasks, and just be there as we push through it. Paradoxically, it seems that we cannot ask for that help, don't know how to, or don't recognize that we need it at the time. We have to rely on others' sensitivity and kindness. Often, miraculously, it is there for us.

I don't know which would have been better: to go through Brent's things right away or to have had the choice to take our time with that task. There are probably advantages either way; regardless, it was a brutal task. It had a dreadful feeling of finality to it, and we felt like we were invading his privacy. I found myself wondering whether he would need this item or that, always snapping back to the reality that he was gone. Yet it was comforting to give close family and friends something of his to keep. There is great comfort there. Now ten years later, I still occasionally wear an item of his clothes.

I was immediately grateful that I had no major regrets. That helped a lot. It's understandable why some people focus on their regrets, but I didn't find myself doing that. We're all on our own journey, doing the best we can, and looking back with regrets doesn't help. Certainly, I was not the perfect mother, and Brent and I hadn't had a perfect relationship. He and I were a lot alike in personality, and that meant we butted heads frequently; but within minutes, we always made amends.

Bob and I had included the boys in most of our travel as a couple, plus I'd done mother-son trips with both Brad and Brent, individually and together. We shared many wonderful and unique experiences. It was an education for them and, in my mind, partially made up for the significant amount of work-related travel I had to do. I'd been able to arrange things so that I made it to most of their events. Bob taught elementary school and coached their sports as they grew up, so his schedule more closely mirrored that of the boys'. Bottom line: Brent knew he was loved and that we were proud of him.

Chapter 6

Coming Home to a Crazy Week

I REMINDED MYSELF that we still had Brad's high school graduation ahead of us, something he was entitled to celebrate, as difficult as that would be. My emotions were all over the place. I wondered, "How do you bury one son and see the other graduate in the same week?"

I began to worry about details. Had all of our family and friends been notified about Brent? We knew this kind of news spreads like wildfire.

I had no idea how many might come for the funeral and where they would stay. I couldn't handle worrying about that; my brain was functioning in slow motion. It occurred to me that there might be one good thing in the timing of all this: some family members arriving for Brent's funeral might want to come early to attend Brad's graduation. But what was I going to do about the house, the food for three events that week, Brad's friends, and our friends and family?

We got off the long flight and found my small car, still parked at the airport form my business trip, a lifetime ago.

Somehow, we managed, barely, to force ourselves and all the luggage into it and start for home. Several friends were waiting there when we arrived. Organized by Kimm, they'd cleaned up the house, done laundry, and made beds; they'd even prepared food for us.

I remember asking later, grinning amidst the grief, "Who cleaned Brad's room?" It was a typical boy's room. Laundry was in piles under his bed and all over his room along with papers, CDs, and lots of dust. I felt a twinge of embarrassment, but that gave way to a chuckle when I saw the faces of my girlfriends. Kimm was single and Fontaine had small children; nether had firsthand experience with a teenage boy's domain. They decided it would be best to wear rubber gloves while they cleared out old paper, food, and crumpled underwear from under the bed.

I think I remember hearing a reference to a stack of off-color magazines somewhere too. I was beginning to realize what wonderful friends we had—especially those we'd made through our involvement with local theater. In these early days of our loss, they were there when we needed them to just listen and offer support; and they were not judgmental.

When we first arrived home, our friends wanted to hear the details of what had happened. As tired as we were, we needed to tell them. My sister and her family were there too, and some of Brad's friends showed up and hung around. They were all trying to support us, and we appreciated that. We picked at food as we let our story pour out. Bob and I alternated, each sharing part of the long weekend in Arizona or chiming in to add something. Brad had taken off with friends—needing to do his own thing.

We felt our first twinges of being overprotective. We had already begun to fear things that had the potential to harm him. We hadn't been separated over the last several days, so when he went to go for a drive with his girlfriend, Krystal, and one of his best friends, Patrick, it was hard to let him go. And yet I understood that I could not stop him; he was nineteen! I knew that he needed to be with his own friends, like we did. I guess I realized, for the first time and with a stab of fear, that I could not really protect my remaining son. Suddenly, many things became tangible threats. I'd never been a worrier, but I was now. This was just one glimpse of how my life was about to change.

After a while, it became obvious that we were tired, so friends helped us clean up and left us be alone as a family. Each one gave us a long hug before leaving. That first night back from Arizona, the loss of Brent really started to set in even though he had never lived in this house full-time—only some weekends and parts of summers. As tired as we were, neither Bob nor I could sleep until we knew that Brad was safe at home. While we waited for him, we sat in the darkened living room, talking about what we'd just been through. We spoke about what we'd had to deal with that week, how we thought Brad was handling it, and just cried with each other.

A little while later, Brad came home. He said he understood we'd be worried about him, and he worried about us too. He seemed a little too relaxed, but we didn't ask any questions, though we had our suspicions. We couldn't be angry at him. Whatever he might have smoked or drank was a minor transgression in the scheme of things. We knew he needed to find temporary comfort in whatever way he could as long as he didn't depend on it as a long-term strategy or endanger anyone. We felt we needed to cut him some slack. For a few minutes, we caught up on the evening's events, and then all of us headed up to bed. I don't think that any of us slept much that night.

The following day, the next level of reality set in. We had to prepare for and organize the rest of the week. We faced daunting tasks, like choosing a cemetery plot, picking out a headstone, deciding the wake, and funeral arrangements—things no one should have to do for their child. We also needed to coordinate with family and friends who were arriving from out of town.

I hadn't the energy to check phone messages when we got home Tuesday night. Wednesday morning, though it was a struggle to get out of bed, I managed to rise and make coffee. I wondered how I managed to do anything that was routine or "normal." Everything was different now; Brent was gone. I started to listen to the phone messages and froze when I heard his voice. Brent left a message for me the night before his accident, reminding me to transfer his monthly allotment of funds. I must have rewound that message and listened to his voice twenty times. It made me cry, but I was so very grateful that at least I had his voice to keep. Then Bob and I listened to it together, bringing us to tears again. You hold on to any tangible shred of your child when they're gone; any little thing that makes you feel closer to them and provide some comfort. I finally got past that message, careful not to delete it, and listened to the others, mostly from friends and family extending their sympathies. It was hard to listen to them, but it was nice to know we had people thinking of us, praying for us, and planning to join us at his service.

Bob and I felt paralyzed, wondering how to begin dealing

with all that we had to do. It was so hard to function, hard to even think clearly. Even Gizmo, the boys' dog, a cute little silver-and-black miniature schnauzer seemed off-kilter. She seemed to know something was wrong, and she was sticking to us like glue. Everywhere we went, she followed and lay at our feet. The night before, when we came home, instead of being her usual exuberant self greeting us, wiggling, and barking, she'd been subdued. As we came up the inside entry stairs, she sat on the step ahead of us, not moving, her head down. Since we'd been home, we'd found her several times in Brent's room, sitting there alone. Could she really know what had happened? It seemed obvious that she did.

Continuing to drink coffee and not caring much about eating, we started to make a list of all the things we had to do during the week ahead: call the priest, reserve the church, make sure Brent's body had arrived from Arizona and had been picked up by our funeral director. Hank was a good person, professional and compassionate. He had also handled my mother's funeral. We had to schedule and go over the details for the wake and funeral. We needed to get Brent's army dress uniform to Hank, pick out flowers and songs, decide who would give readings and who would present the eulogy.

I broke down again thinking about having to pick out a cemetery plot. I hated the thought of putting Brent into the ground, but I hated the thought of cremating him even more. We had to make sure all our close family and friends were informed about the specifics of the wake and funeral and that they would pass on the information to others. We had to get ready for Laura and her parents who would be staying with us. We had family and friends coming from several states, and they would have to make their own arrangements. We couldn't worry about that; we were barely functioning.

It was so hard to think in any kind of logical, coherent fashion. I felt stupid. I couldn't listen to music, I couldn't read for any length of time, I couldn't focus on anything. I worried that I was experiencing some sort of mental illness or disability. I thought, "Would I get better or have to live with this for the rest of my life? Is this normal?"

Brad was still sleeping—poor guy, he must have been exhausted. Bob and I showered, dressed, fed Gizmo, and headed out to deal with our list of tasks. I wondered if we had forgotten anything. And then it occurred to me: Brad was graduating from high school tomorrow! I wondered what that must be like for him. Bob and I agreed that we had to do something to make his experience as "normal" as possible. Despite the horror of his brother's death, Brad didn't deserve to have his graduation totally ruined; it was a big accomplishment. So we added additional items to our list: notify friends and family about the graduation and arrange some simple catering for a small party afterward. We decided to get a cake, one with a message of congratulations on it. What a remarkable contrast in feelings all in the same week: great happiness and deep pride for Brad because he had finished high school and was heading to college, but in the same week we were burying his brother.

At the top of the list was meeting with Hank. He had a beautiful home on Newburyport's High Street, which was noted in many architectural textbooks as a street containing a magnificent array of old Federalist architecture and stately sea captain's homes. Hank and his family lived above his funeral parlor in one of those homes. The house, white with burgundy shutters and trim, was set back from the street at the crest of a hill with a beautiful sloping green lawn and trees in front.

We pulled into his long driveway and parked in the back, knocking on his private entrance door as he'd suggested. Hank greeted us, and we were invited into his office where he made us comfortable; he knew this process was very difficult. Although we didn't know him well, we were grateful that we had some connection. Hank was a good friend of my sister and brother-in-law, and we'd talked with him at various events.

Bob handed Brent's army dress uniform to Hank, whose eyes filled with tears. He shook his head slowly as if to say no, hung the uniform out of sight, and placed a box of tissues in front of us, asking how we were doing. He warned us that this conversation was going to be a difficult one.

Hank confirmed that he would pick up Brent's body that evening at the airport. Brent would be ready for a service that weekend. It was comforting knowing that Brent's remains were being handled by friends who cared.

We arrived at the horrible moment when we needed to choose a casket for our son. We hadn't planned on any of this expense, but we knew it had to be a really nice quality wooden one—one that Brent would have been proud of. That seemed silly and necessary at the same time; it wasn't logical, but in the end, cost didn't matter. We were just trying to do what we thought our son would like. He'd be laid out for the wake in a good-looking casket in his army dress uniform. Oddly enough, army green had been his favorite color since he was a kid. The casket was a lovely medium dark oak with a reddish brown hue lined with cream-colored satin. We wanted him to feel pride even now; we'd worry how to pay for all this later.

We mentioned our plan to see the priest at the Immaculate Conception church about holding the funeral service there. None of us were looking forward to that conversation; all of us had experienced the lack of flexibility this church parish had when it came to customizing a service to reflect family preferences. Hank made it clear he would do whatever we wanted, but he suggested that we have the "sharing" service idea from Arizona as part of the wake rather than the funeral. Tearfully, and making use of the tissues Hank had provided, we talked through the details of the wake and funeral, Friday and Saturday, only two days away. We thought that the dates we had chosen would make it easier on our out-of-state guests who would then be able to use Sunday as a travel day. We also needed to get this behind us. I now understood that just pushing onward kept the numbness we felt from turning into other, more deeply painful emotions at first. One foot in front of the other; check off one task at a time—it was all we could do, all we could handle.

These deadlines provided focus. We needed that. It literally gave us something to get out of bed for. We talked through the tentative plan for Hank's interactions with the church around the funeral and agreed we'd check back with him after we'd spoken to the priest.

Hank recounted a near-death experience of his own, trying to comfort us with his story of how he felt so wonderful crossing over that it was hard for him to come back. He said that he was no longer afraid of dying; he believed that all of our spirits live on, including Brent's. While this topic felt strange to us, his story was comforting and gave us hope.

I had no idea what I thought about an afterlife. Before Brent's death, I had never really been forced to think about it. I'd wondered about it over the years. Catholicism, the faith in which I'd been raised, supported the idea of an afterlife, as did most major religions I knew of. I'd assumed both my parents and my innocent stillborn son Robbie went to heaven, but I didn't have the burning desire to confirm an afterlife until Brent died. Perhaps I needed to find confirmation that Brent was all right. I'd been programmed as a parent to protect him, but I was no longer able to do that. I wanted to hear anything that gave me hope that he lived on.

We wrapped up our discussion by ordering small memorial cards with Brent's picture and a poem that we'd chosen from one of the sympathy cards we'd received. Hank also gave us thank-you cards to send out later.

We headed to the church for our appointment. We'd asked to meet with the younger priest at the Immaculate Conception church where so many of my family religious events had taken place. It seemed right to have Brent's funeral in the place we'd held his first Holy Communion and where we attended family weddings and funerals. I didn't get along very well with the current pastor; I found him very rigid, placing too many restrictions on personally significant services. We'd already butted heads over my mother's funeral. I'd hoped the young priest would be more flexible, and it seemed appropriate to have a young priest say Brent's funeral Mass.

But when we met with him, we quickly discovered that he was aligned with the church's position of inflexibility, something he freely admitted. He told us that any music had to be selected from a short list of "acceptable" hymns. He also told us that the church preferred no eulogy but would tolerate one eulogy by one person that did not exceed five minutes. There could be only two readings, selected from their pamphlet although there were a few from the Bible that they deemed "appropriate." They would not allow any sort of "sharing" during the ceremony. We were also reminded that an appropriate donation was required to cover church, priests, and altar boys. And we were expected to provide flowers on the altar, but we could also choose to place flowers in other locations in the church.

We had our own ideas about what we wanted for our son's funeral. It was very important to us to make it special and unique to him, choosing our own readings and music. We'd found the simple sharing done by Brent's friends in the service out in Arizona to have had magical, healing qualities, and we especially wanted to include something like that in this service.

"This is my son's funeral," I said to the priest. "We should be able to honor him in any way *we* feel appropriate."

But he wouldn't soften his position. We thought about changing the funeral to another church, one in the next town. The priest was friendly and open-minded there; we'd spoken to him in our consideration of it. But in the end, our family church was much more beautiful and felt right because so many of family events had taken place there. Besides that, I'd grown up going to this church, so tradition won out. We grudgingly agreed to compromise and got the priest to compromise a little, and we moved the sharing session to the wake. We selected biblical readings and dropped off a CD with a Jane Sibbery and K. D. Lang song,

"Calling All Angels" from the movie *Pay It Forward*. The priest insisted on screening the song before agreeing.

I felt like screaming at him, "Aren't you supposed to be comforting us? Are your 'policies' more important than offering solace to a grieving parent?" His priorities seemed very detached from the enormity of this situation. He was insensitive to us and ultimately to what Brent would have wanted. I expressed muted displeasure in a mumbled, "You're not serious!" then forced myself to walk away. This part would be over soon enough. We would still be able to close out Brent's life on earth with a ceremony that would take place in a church that was important to us. It would have pleased my parents, Brent's grandparents—no longer with us.

From there, we headed over to the cemetery to pick out Brent's burial plot and to Newburyport Memorial Art Company to pick out his gravestone.

We looked at two local cemeteries, to decide which would be the best for the final resting place of our son. We visited Pine Hill cemetery first; it was old, with rolling hills and tons of local history. Many prominent figures were buried there. The remaining area that still had space for new plots was near a busy street and well within distance of an extremely unpleasant odor from a nearby farm, which I knew would appear periodically. I couldn't deal with that and imagined it would get worse at the height of summer heat. The one we chose, St Mary's, is a pleasant, medium-sized Catholic graveyard at the north end of town. It was where my parents and our younger son Robbie were buried. We met with the caretaker who told us they were opening up plots in one of two places: near a side street, which was closer to my family, or in the back, adjacent to and overlooking a local golf course. We chose the latter because it was quieter, and because Brent had become a golf fanatic. We thought he'd like that resting place better.

The question arose: how many plots should we buy? Bob and I did not have our own yet. Do we buy one just for Brent and leave him alone? Do we buy four, one for each of us in the family? We settled on three, figuring that Brad would probably have his own family and want a plot with his future wife. Even if Brad did want to be buried with his brother, Bob was pretty sure he wanted to be cremated; his ashes could share a plot with Brent or me. You just don't think about this until you are forced to.

With the decision made and still feeling that this process wasn't real, we next went to look at gravestones. It was hard to visualize our son's name etched on a headstone, so permanent and cold. At the same time, we wanted it well done and unique. Friends and family would visit him here, and his stone is the only thing they'd be able to see or touch.

When I first walked in, leaning against the small building on the ground to the right of a big open garage door, I noticed a small gray ragged piece of granite with the striking black outline of a swallowtail butterfly on it, roughly a foot square. I recognized the butterfly as a symbol of transition, something I'd already begun to think a lot about. I mentally held on to that image as we moved on, waiting to speak to the owner who was busy helping someone else. Meanwhile, we looked through the many large and small headstones that were on display in the adjacent yard. It was difficult to choose, but we wanted this to be a nice tribute. Because we now owned three plots, we felt that we needed a large marker. We could have ordered a custom-made stone, but that would take too much time, and we wanted to get this completed. Finally, we chose a handsome salmon-and-gray granite headstone, neither gaudy nor elaborate, which was large enough. Two decorative columns of leaves were carved vertically in the front with space to accommodate family names and a quote. The backside of it would hold a short tribute and Brent's name, allowing space for the names of those who would someday occupy the other plots. We talked about moving Robbie's body, which was buried with my parents, to be with his older brother. But in the end, we decided that it was too disruptive and chose to have his name and dates engraved on the back of the stone below Brent's. It would offer us a symbolic way to bring them together. It is interesting to see what becomes important to you as you go through this process.

Bob wanted something patriotic etched onto the stone to reflect Brent's passion for the military, so we chose an American flag waving on a pole. The flag displayed the stars and stripes. I remembered the butterfly image and asked that both the butterfly and the flag be rendered in the same smaller size and placed on opposite corners at the top rear of the stone, above Brent and Robbie's names and dates. On the front, under the family name, we had the following quote engraved: "Though the voice is quiet, the spirit echoes still."

The stone would be installed within a couple weeks after the funeral, when the ground was firm and the cemetery staff had poured a cement foundation to hold the heavy granite piece. We wanted to mark Brent's grave as soon as possible and found that quotation comforting.

I sympathize with parents whose child dies during the

winter, when the ground is frozen, and they must wait for this simple but important acknowledgement of their child.

Finished with this task, we stopped to get some groceries and headed home, once again emotionally and physically exhausted. We found it difficult to focus on the mundane and probably only got part of what we needed, but no one cared. We also needed to check in with Brad. After we got home, friends and family began to drop in to offer condolences, some arriving from other states. My sister's family came over; we sat for a long time talking about Brent, intermixing laughter and tears. We were a close family. My nieces Stacey and Kim, first cousins to Brent and Brad, were devastated. We helped each other through it. We dug out the duffel bags we'd brought home from Arizona and allowed them each to pick out something of Brent's to keep. They seemed to appreciate that—a way of holding on to him.

We confirmed the details of Brad's graduation the following day with them and called close friends to do the same. They were all going to attend; Hope, one of my nieces' friends, had even come up from South Carolina for both the graduation and the funeral. My sister agreed to pick up the cake and help with the food. We were so grateful for their help. This long day ended, and they all went home to my sister's house while we retired for another restless night.

The next morning, we tried to put on happy faces and congratulate Brad on his high school graduation, and we made sure everything he needed had been provided. We'd encouraged him to invite friends back to the house for a small party. We really wanted to celebrate his achievement as much as possible. As it turned out, nearly twenty family and friends attended his graduation ceremony that evening. Sitting together in the stands, we were the group cheering the loudest when he was called up to receive his diploma. He needed that even though he was probably embarrassed by our enthusiasm. Brad said that he was glad to be finished with high school. Grief-stricken, he said having others around helped.

After we had taken a few pictures with him in his cap and gown, we headed back to the house. More friends arrived, and everyone pitched in to help. Laura and her parents brought Tom, Brent's roommate, with them from Arizona, generously providing for his flight ticket. It meant a lot to us that that they'd all come so far to honor Brent. After they carried their luggage upstairs and settled in, they joined the group.

We were pretty successful in keeping the mood light for Brad's party, and we took some great pictures of him and his close friends. They were protective of him, and that was nice to see. They remain a good group of young people.

As the party wound down and the crowd thinned out, we started to plan for the wake. Talk about a change in mood! Hank had placed a notice in the local paper, which included an invitation to speak at Brent's sharing service near the end of the wake. We put out calls through our communication trees to make sure family and friends knew; it was all happening very quickly.

We pored over many of our old photo albums and pulled out pictures of Brent with family and friends at different ages to make a collage. That was a painful task. We sat on the living room floor and talked with Laura's family as we went through the photographs, often in tears. After a while, we decided to put the collage together in the morning, so we hugged and headed to bed. It had been quite a day but lovely to have people around us who cared.

Friday morning, we woke up early; we still had a great deal to do. People continued to arrive from out of town. We were all trying to get showered—with limited hot water—dressed, and grab some breakfast. We put out a simple breakfast, for everyone to help themselves. I worked on the three photo collage boards for the wake until Bob's family arrived from New Jersey and Pennsylvania, and there was yet another tearful exchange of stories and memories.

We continued to give each family member something of Brent's as a keepsake. They had also brought pictures of Brent with them. My sister's family dropped in to see if they could help. Friends called to offer condolences and assistance.

In the midst of the chaos, as we were getting ready to leave for the family-only portion of the wake, an understanding friend—Anna—called and asked if we'd like her husband Alan to videotape the sharing portion of the wake. I hadn't thought of that; the idea seemed a little odd at first, but I figured why not? It might be good to have later. I accepted her offer and thanked her. I've been grateful ever since and watch it every year.

Leaving the house reasonably neat, since guests would be back later, we gathered our things and piled into a few cars. We left the door unlocked because Kimm and her army of our friends were coming to set up food for after the wake. It was a great relief knowing that all those details were being handled by our dear friends. We drove the few miles to the funeral home preparing ourselves to see our son in uniform in his casket for the first time.

Hank escorted our family into the room where Brent's body was laid out in his casket, clad in his army dress greens and medals. We may have thought we were prepared, but it was a shock. He looked pale but peaceful and handsome. His shirt collar and the knot of his tie covered the scar where they'd intubated him at the scene of the accident. Hank had done a good job, but our children never look the same once life has left them. It isn't their closed eyes or the cosmetic attempt to restore their healthy color, but rather that their spirit, the essence of who they are, is no longer there.

It was very upsetting to see Brent this way. I cried silently, trying to be strong for the others who I knew were behind me and watching as I knelt at his side. I felt faint as I reached to touch him; a kiss from my lips on my fingertips I placed on his cheek. It was cold; his body was stiff and cold. I gasped slightly and thought, "Oh my God, is this really Brent?"

Bob knelt beside me to the left; I could feel him shaking, trying to keep from breaking down entirely. Brad was standing at my right, his hand on my shoulder. I could tell he too was on thin ice emotionally. Brent had been such a big presence in our lives, regardless of whether he lived near or far from us, that we couldn't imagine life without him.

After a few minutes that seemed like an eternity, they helped me up, and we moved away to let other family members view Brent before the wake opened to the public. Each successive family group that went up to the casket struggled to believe what they were seeing after last seeing

Brent so vibrant and alive. Everyone was struggling with their emotions.

We started to mingle and talk amongst ourselves. Hank got us some water and tissues. About fifteen minutes before the wake began, the priest from the Catholic church came and offered a blessing. It was standard fare, by the book, no surprise. Hank asked us if we were ready to let the public join us and indicated that a line had formed outside. We agreed to start although we weren't sure what to expect from people or how we'd feel witnessing their reaction to Brent. It is such a shock when a young person dies unexpectedly, like Brent; but I assume that even after a long illness, a young person's funeral is still shocking for family and friends.

We were amazed at how many people showed up. For more than three hours, they kept coming, filling the entire main floor and multiple side rooms of the funeral home. It was heartwarming to see such an outpouring of love and respect for Brent and for us. People came that I hadn't seen in years, parents of the friends he'd made growing up, parents of old girlfriends, our close friends, neighbors, work colleagues, and acquaintances from organizations or events around town. Extended family and others came from quite a distance, including New Hampshire, Maine, New York, New Jersey, Pennsylvania, Virginia, South Carolina, and of course, Arizona. It was wonderful to see them all.

As is customary, the immediate family formed a receiving line just beyond the casket to greet people after they'd had a chance to spend a moment with Brent. At first, it was extremely difficult, and I did lots of hugging and crying with everyone who passed. Eventually, it was easier to talk to them and hear their stories about Brent, even laugh with them, which generated some strange looks that I noticed.

We shared stories about the time Brent fell down a cement storm drain near a construction site, coming home bleeding from a gash under his arm. He was using his brother's shirt as a makeshift tourniquet. And the time, he'd tried to saw a large bowling ball in half, slipped and cut his arm, narrowly missing a major artery. Bob rushed him to the emergency room, leaving me with a house full of out-of-state relatives waiting for my mother to arrive for a surprise seventy-fifth birthday party. Thankfully, my aunt was able to stall her until we got the news that Brent was all right.

Perhaps the story that most typified Brent was the time I had to bring both boys to the emergency room at the same time because of a series of bumps and bruises that alarmed even the emergency room staff.

Brent had tackled Brad on a cement playground, breaking Brad's collarbone, requiring him to wear a shoulder brace. A day or two later, when Brent could run around and Brad could not, Brent kept slapping Brad on the head when he passed him. Brad tripped Brent in retaliation, causing him to crash into heavy furniture, developing a large black forehead bump and two black eyes. The next day, Brent leapt off the uppermost bar of his swing set and broke his wrist. I was home alone with them and had to take them both into the ER where the staff saw all this as well as the normal bruises Brent always had from playing. They felt compelled to pull Brent aside to assess whether the injuries were the result of abuse. He was very creative even at a young age and, under normal circumstances might have made up a story, placing me in big trouble; but luckily he didn't understand.

The laughter from sharing these and other memories provided tremendously needed moments of relief. I suppose conventional behavior advises against laughing at a wake, but I found it very healing. These people cared about Brent, and showed it.

Afterward, knowing a sibling loss was very different from the kind of loss Bob and I were feeling, I asked how Brad had experienced the wake. Brad is an introvert and dislikes being the center of attention, which is unavoidable in these circumstances. For him, having to stand and endure the many expressions of sympathy was horrible. He already felt bad enough; he just wanted to go home and do nothing, to be by himself. What was comforting to me—the condolences of others—was not at all comforting to him. We all grieve differently.

Instead of holding the wake for four hours, we'd cut it back to three and said we'd conclude with a "sharing session." That would continue until everyone who wanted to had a chance to speak. After three hours, there were still two rooms filled with people wanting to participate in some way. A sound system allowed everyone to hear, regardless of where they sat. There was a lectern with a small microphone to the right of the casket. Hank went to the lectern and welcomed anyone to speak, indicating that Bob and I would go first.

Because Bob would give the eulogy at the funeral, I began. I did not have anything prepared, just spoke from my heart and told the story about Brent being so adventurous, riding his bike down our neighbors' driveway while standing on the middle bar without holding on. It was so typically Brent, an example of how he liked to experience life. I heard sympathetic chuckles. I explained how lucky I felt to have had wonderful sons like him and Brad and how much we'd miss Brent as well as how much we appreciated everyone's support. This was going to be the hardest journey I'd ever been on, but I was trying to find something positive to say, and I think I managed to do that.

Bob followed me with some notes he'd written. He looked crushed when he stepped up the podium, tired with red and swollen eyes. He spoke eloquently for a few minutes, talking from the heart about the tragedy of a young life cut short; it was just an accident after all. There was no one to blame; he'd miss his son terribly. You could hear sniffles in the room.

Brent had had a strong interest in theater, and most of our friends in the theater knew him quite well, so they were present. Our friend Andre Dubus III, a NY Times best-selling and award-winning author, sent us an extremely touching three-page handwritten letter immediately after he heard about Brent.

I'd asked Andre to read the letter at the sharing service and called him up to do so. Andre has an amazing energized presence; it was wonderful to hear him read his tribute to Brent, capturing Brent's love of life and self-confidence. I was very grateful; I still have that letter.

We opened up the sharing part of the service, and gradually, family and friends came to the podium to speak. Some were shy and slightly uncomfortable, some were funny, some were sad, but their comments were all heartfelt. It was an amazing tribute to Brent; I cannot imagine a better one.

One theme came through loud and clear: how competitive Brent was. Laura's father told an amusing story about playing golf with Brent who, despite being behind in his score, retained a cockiness that he could win a "new nine." Laura spoke about the countless games of pool she'd played with him, losing most of them, but she put up with it because she loved being with him. His friend Tom talked about how he and Brent played many games of video football. Brent wouldn't quit until he finally beat Tom. Once that happened, the game lost its allure, and Brent didn't need to play anymore. The ultimate expression of his fierce competitive spirit was during a New Year's Eve party at our home. Brent ended up in a good-natured wresting match on the floor with our friend Deb, who was in a long dress, over the contents of a party piñata; then he initiated an arm-wrestling contest. By far, the most intense match was between Brent and his father. I can't even remember who won, but it was pretty entertaining to watch, and these memories were lovely to hear from others.

All these wonderful people shared from their hearts, and others who didn't speak stayed to listen, which also meant a great deal to us. I felt gratitude to everyone who attended, sent letters and books, brought food, called and offered support, or just listened. It was a generous outpouring; and in spite of my deep grief, I felt loved, supported, and blessed. I was so grateful that I'd been inspired by the service in Arizona to include this wonderful sharing of memories, and I was also grateful that our friend Alan captured it on video.

While we sat packed into two rooms set up with rows of chairs and a narrow aisle, the sharing session went on for almost two hours. There were so many stories about

Brent, so many tears and laughter. Bob, Brad, and I sat to the left of the podium in front of Brent's casket. Every speaker acknowledged Brent and hugged us before they returned to their seats.

There was so much love and empathy in that room. Finally, when everyone had spoken, the Congregational minister and a friend, Kent Allen, stepped up to close the wake. I hadn't even realized he'd been there listening to the entire session until he summarized so eloquently what he'd heard about Brent. I was stunned and held Bob's and Brad's hands as I listened. Even though Kent had never met Brent, he wove elements of what everyone had said into a wonderful tribute to Brent—what a gift to us. I was filled with gratitude for his participation and skill; it was comforting in a unique way. Kent then said a lovely and impromptu prayer from his heart. After that, we asked Hank to invite everyone back to our home.

By now it was nearly 9:00 PM on a Friday, and yet several friends and family returned to the house with us. Kimm and some of my other girlfriends had organized food and drink in a buffet. She wouldn't let me help with anything, and so we were relieved of kitchen and hosting duty, which gave me precious time to sit and talk with guests. On that beautiful, warm June night overlooking the ocean, we sat on the deck under the stars, our conversation punctuated by the gentle sound of the waves.

I remember having some deep discussions about life and death. I also spent time telling colleagues from work who'd never met him, about Brent. Several times I broke down in tears, but because of the support all around me, I did not feel overwhelmed. Later, after they were gone, things would be different.

Along the deck railing, overlooking the water, we had placed a line of glowing citronella candles. After much reminiscing and a little wine, our guests departed. Bob blew out the candles, and we headed to bed. But first, he made one last trip downstairs to make sure the candles were out and the door locked. We got into bed and tried to sleep.

Since Brent's death, I'd been restless and had difficulty sleeping. Insomnia was not usual for me. Normally, I could sleep just about anywhere at any time, undisturbed by any amount of noise. But not now. Something made me snap open my eyes in the middle of this night. I felt a presence and saw, in the darkened room, tiny moving dots of light. In my peripheral vision, I saw something cloudy, and it was moving. Was I still sleeping? I blinked a few times to make sure I was awake, but the lights were still there. Something compelled me to get up and go downstairs, walking quietly to avoid awakening anyone. In the combined open living and dining room, the moon shone in through the large windows at the back of the house, making an eerie glow. Then I noticed it: one of the candles was still burning. I couldn't believe my eyes. If I had blown the candles out, I might have missed one and just written it off. But Bob had a touch of OCD that made him good at locking up or being careful around fire, so I knew he'd double-checked the candles. Was this a sign from my son? I went out on the deck, feeling what I believed was Brent's presence. After a moment, I said good night to him and blew the candle out, tears streaming down my cheeks. I felt so much love for him and at the same time so much grief. Exhausted, but still not sleepy, I made myself go back upstairs to lie down. I lay awake, thinking about the funeral, a few hours from then.

I kept waking up, reliving the night before and anticipating the day ahead. Bob was restless too, but it was too much effort for us to speak.

We got up early, showered, and went downstairs to make coffee and a simple breakfast for guests. There wasn't much time; we had to get to the funeral home for a final farewell before the casket was closed and the pallbearers put it into the hearse to be taken to the church. Each of us brought something to place in the casket before it was closed. The three of us and Laura also wanted a few minutes alone with Brent. We arrived before 9:00 AM, and Hank led us into the quiet, chilly room where Brent was laid out. We stood together in front of the casket and, one at a time, leaned over Brent and said our final good-byes. This was a terrible, painful moment. We were crying; my knees trembled. I felt barely able to stand.

Together, we placed Freddy—the small worn teddy bear Brent had since he was an infant—in his arms. I'd bought Freddy, a machine washable toy, when Brent was born, and he loved it. He took it to bed with him and nearly everywhere else. Freddy wore a tattered blue bib with a red apple in the center, which my mother had repaired several times, and his fur was worn in spots. Freddy had always been part of the family—the only real baby toy of Brent's that hadn't been given or thrown away. He belonged with Brent, but it was hard to let him go. Bob leaned over to put in Brent's baseball glove and kiss Brent on the forehead - then he broke down; it was so hard to witness. Brad then leaned over Brent and put a poker chip in his breast pocket from when they'd been in Las Vegas together. He'd kept it as a souvenir. He held onto his brother's arm, his face wet, which was even harder to watch. Going last, I put in one of my favorite scarves, a shell from the beach in front of our house and Brent's maroon-and-gold ASU lanyard keychain.

Sobbing and leaning on the casket, I couldn't bear to say this last good-bye. And then for one final time, I kissed his forehead and caressed his face and arms.

How could we bury our son? How could we leave him?

Then Hank came in to ask if he could close the casket and open the room to the family and pallbearers. And then it was time to offer the final prayer before taking Brent to the church.

We left the room for a few minutes, and when we returned, the casket was closed. This was very unsettling. Hank led a short prayer and then guided us out through the front door into a limo, which would lead other waiting cars. Then he went back inside to help the pallbearers wheel the casket toward the doors.

Brent had eight pallbearers rather than the customary six. They included his father and brother; his uncles Paul, John, and Frank; and our friends Kyle and Sam plus his roommate Tom—all people who loved Brent. Carefully, I later learned, they lifted Brent's casket off the gurney and slid it into the back of the hearse. I'm glad I didn't see that. I waited in the limo with Laura and her family.

We drove to Immaculate Conception church and waited for the others to enter. The pallbearers went to the back of the hearse, and we went inside where we waited in the rear vestibule. From there, I could see the inside of the church and the outside curb and street through the open doors. I noticed the church was filled, which was comforting. I was still shaky, and when the pall bearers carried Brent's casket in from the hearse, setting it atop the wheeled gurney at the back of the church, I broke down and sobbed.

We'd asked Laura and Brent's godparents—my sister Pat and her husband Paul—to assist Bob, Brad, and me with the ritual of spreading the beautiful gold-and-white pall over the top of the casket. We did so silently, each lingering with hands on the casket for a few seconds. Once finished, the others filed in and sat down in the reserved family area. I was supported by Bob and Brad on either side of me as we walked down the center aisle to the front pew on the right. Laura and her parents and my sister's family were behind us.

The funeral procession began with altar boys in cassocks, carrying a large wooden crucifix, the vessels for the Mass, followed by the young priest and the pastor. Because of our discussions about the funeral with the younger clergyman, the pastor called me to ask if he could assist in the service without leading it. I agreed. I'm sure he was shocked at our earlier request that he not lead the service, but he deserves credit for still wanting to take part in it.

On his way to the altar, the priest shook incense in the air around the casket, which triggered a strong reaction in me—the pungent and familiar smell evoking my history with Catholic ceremony. They said Mass, dedicating it to Brent. My sister and I went up to the pulpit and each gave a reading I had selected. Bob read his eulogy, which was very touching and emotional. It meant a lot to him to be the one to deliver it. Brad and I sat with arms locked in the front pew, watching his father, who was both proud of Brent and in great pain.

We'd selected four songs: "Amazing Grace," "Time to Say Good-bye," "Calling All Angels," and "Ave Maria." The latter had special meaning to us since it had often been used at family weddings and funerals.

And so we were finally, after an intense week, bringing some things to closure and approaching the formal ending of our son's life.

It was difficult to hear the priest discuss Brent in the past tense. He then said the benediction that concluded the Mass. He said that internment would follow at St. Mary's Cemetery and then a gathering at our home. I wept before standing up to leave this lovely but sad service.

The priests and altar boys led the recessional followed by the other pallbearers bringing Brent's casket then Bob, Brad, and I, touching the casket when it was within reach. Behind us were the rest of our family and friends. The casket was lifted into the hearse, and we headed to the limo. Everyone else scattered to their cars. As we walked out of the church, I leaned on Bob and Brad again. I think we were all holding each other up. There was such sadness in the faces of everyone we passed. It was a blur. I can't even remember everyone who was there, but I was grateful for their support.

I have a clear memory of glancing at Laura when we were seated in the limo and thinking that she looked like she was barely hanging on. I can only imagine what she must have been feeling—the future she had planned vanished in one day. It's heartbreaking when young love with so much promise is so abruptly ended. Laura's sadness made me think back to when I first met her. She looked so beautiful and happy then.

Brent had called home one evening saying he'd met a new girl, Laura, at a party on campus. He spoke differently about her than he had about other girls. He was more deliberate in his choice of words; he spoke more slowly, and it seemed his voice had a deeper resonance. In the past, his descriptions were limited to a girl's looks or how receptive she was to him or what she thought about him. This time, he talked more about his feelings, and while he mentioned Laura's appearance, it was with a certain reverence and a much-deeper appreciation. She'd become more important than his own ego, which was quite an accomplishment. Within a week, over the phone, even from across the country, I could tell that he'd become monogamous. This was rare for Brent, who normally dated several young women at the same time. Laura really meant something to him, and I was eager to meet her.

Not long after that, Brent brought Laura home for a visit, and when we picked them up at Logan airport in Boston, we saw what Brent had seen in her; she won us all over immediately. Back then, we could still meet passengers at the gate. My son came off the plane proud and beaming, ready to show off his new love. Laura, holding his hand, was smiling but quiet, probably nervous about meeting us.

I greeted them both with hugs, a little more carefully with Laura so I wouldn't overwhelm her. It was always so good to see Brent. We didn't get to see him enough since he'd moved away.

Laura was approximately five foot seven, in good shape, with long straight blond hair, intelligent blue eyes, and beautiful skin with a healthy glow. She wore no makeup; she didn't need it.

I couldn't help but grin. Brent had always been attracted to blonds while his brother was usually attracted to brunettes. Laura's style was simple; she wore jeans and a T-shirt, both soft blues tones, and delicate silver jewelry. Her shoes looked comfortable, and she carried a light jacket.

I could tell immediately that she was more mature and confident than Brent's previous girlfriends. She didn't engage in nervous chatter or veer off on tangents. Laura looked you in the eyes when she spoke, and she was comfortable with natural silences in the conversation. When I asked her about college and her family, it was clear she had a great home life and relationship with her parents. It was evident that she was a quality woman who was intelligent, mature, and had her own interests and career plan. I could see Brent was intrigued and challenged by this woman; he had not found her so easy to influence, and he seemed to realize that. I think he felt Laura was worth the effort it took to maintain a successful relationship. Even at such an early stage, this had a long-term feel to it.

We walked together to retrieve their luggage from the carousel and our car from the parking garage. As we did, I started to get to know this young woman who had already triggered some noticeable changes in my son. I observed him doing little things, like carrying her bag and opening doors for her—putting her first. She'd brought out the gentleman in him, and I loved that.

Brent and Laura climbed into the backseat of the car, and we put their luggage in the trunk. Bob drove; I turned around from the front seat to talk with them. I asked Laura how she and Brent met. She smiled at him, squeezed his hand, and said that they had met on campus at a friend's party. Beaming, Brent chimed in and said that she had been wearing a miniskirt and had great legs, so he'd noticed her right away. He had gone over to talk with her, and they had really hit it off. Laura, grinning as well, added softly that she found Brent cute, with a great smile, and that his friendly confidence when he had offered her a beer had made an impression on her. They had ended up talking to each other the rest of the night. She liked that he was in ROTC and had made plans for his future.

For the entire ride, as I spoke with them, I noticed they held hands and kept glancing at each other; it was sweet.

Laura, an only child, was born in New Jersey but had grown up and lived in Phoenix, Arizona, where she was studying at ASU to be a landscape architect. Though she was two and a half years older than Brent, she was one year ahead of him in college because she'd transferred from Northern Arizona State and changed majors. Laura had done some adventurous things, like driving cross-country with a girlfriend on their own. A dog lover and nurturer, she owned a large male black Lab-and-Chow mix dog named Cain. Laura had rescued him from a shelter and nursed him back to health after his abuse by a previous owner. She also won over Bob and Brad even though they were very different personalities from me. Laura charmed the entire family just by being herself.

Even now, I still feel that way about her—even more so, if that's possible. Laura was like a surrogate daughter, the daughter I'd never had, and I felt her pain.

Slowly, we threaded our way through town to Brent's

final resting place, a long, slow procession of cars led by the hearse and our limo.

We arrived at St. Mary's Cemetery, about three miles from the church, and the long line of cars made its way through the grounds to the back of the cemetery. The cars were like a huge snake with the hearse at its head. We got out and watched the pallbearers bring the casket to the open grave where they set it on a frame, which would later be lowered into the ground. They covered the lid with some of the flowers people had sent to the wake; the other flowers were donated to local nursing homes, and we kept a few for home. People started to gather around the gravesite. I remember greeting them and offering some comfort while trying to maintain my own composure.

The final ceremony started with a rendition of taps, played as a tribute by a young uniformed soldier from the local National Guard. Colonel Crawford, Brent's commanding officer at ASU, had arranged this performance; but I'd forgotten and was shocked by the haunting sound of it. Standing in front of the casket, I held on to Brent and Bob. It was good that I did. Although I am not the type to faint, and don't remember it, I was later told that my knees buckled twice. They caught me, and held me up. I thought I was handling all of this, but apparently, I was overwhelmed. The young man purposely stayed a distance away in respect. Once finished, he simply saluted, nodded, and walked away. Bob ran after him to thank him.

There was a prayer and final words said over the gravesite, and then Hank asked everyone to say their final good-bye to Brent before leaving. I was really struggling not to lose it entirely, and I could see that Bob, Brad, and Laura were shaky too. I held on to Bob and leaned over to pick up a few flowers from atop his casket to take home with me to dry and save. I placed my hands on the casket and, sobbing, said the last good-bye to my son. I didn't want him to be alone, and I wasn't sure I wanted to go on without him. But Bob and Brad needed me; we needed each other. With effort, I stood up, hugged them both, and then watched as they said their good-byes. Leaving Brent was inconceivably painful, but it had to be done.

We didn't want to see him lowered into the ground; we turned to go. Brad said that he was glad he'd been a pallbearer; at least he could do that much for his brother. I don't think any of us said a word on the way home.

When we got home, we were rescued by Kimm and her cadre of our friends who had prepared food and drinks for the crowd that returned with us. It turned out to be a warm, sunny Saturday, and our large deck overlooking the ocean helped us to take full advantage of that pleasant, healing place. We relaxed and talked about Brent and caught up with people we hadn't seen in a long time; some took walks on the beach. I had a short moment of panic when I thought we didn't have enough food, but I was able to pull some things out of the freezer, and then Kimm and company took over. Some people brought wine and beer to supplement our supply, and in the end, it all worked out.

In the primarily Irish family that I was raised in, parties after a wake or funeral were standard. I used to think they were disrespectful until my father died. That made me realize how healing it was to sit with friends and tell stories about the deceased, to feel the support, comfort, and love of those around you.

I found that to be even more important with the loss of a child. We were barely functioning, so having loved ones around us was invaluable—the moral support and assistance with everyday tasks. I didn't know yet how tough it would be when that support thinned out.

It was difficult and yet comforting to continue to share stories, reminding us that Brent was loved and had made an impression. I also reminisced about how often I'd been to the emergency room with both boys and the time the tables were turned. Once, they had to bring me to the ER when I thought I had broken my foot while moving into our current home. We laughed together then about how we'd come full circle in our mother-son ER adventures. I was so grateful for the moments of laughter, which were so healing. It had been a long day. Again, we were physically and emotionally exhausted by the time people headed home. Some of our friends stayed long enough to help us clean up. My sister's family and my in-laws stayed a little longer. Laura, Maureen, Larry, and Tom were staying over one more night; their return flight was Sunday morning. We sat on the deck as a smaller group for a while, talking about life and Brent as well as our plans for the immediate future.

Brad said, "I think the funeral was a good tribute to Brent, but I am worried about what happens when reality really sets in for all of us. It's hard to think about the future without Brent." He looked so sad. I wished I could make his pain go away. Understandably, he was worried about the impact the loss was going to have on him and our family. Brad is pretty intuitive. I wonder now if he foresaw any of our issues coming.

We all finally headed to bed, though we were reluctant to leave each other. We'd been through a very intense experience together. Laura and her family promised to come back and visit us. We also promised to come to Arizona and visit them and stay in touch. We were family now, permanently.

Sunday morning, we got up early again and put on a pot of coffee so we could each draw a cup at our convenience, and we took showers in shifts. We went together for breakfast at Mad Martha's Café across the street. Brad was working at the café part-time then. Later on, he would own that café after he graduated from the culinary program at Johnson and Wales University. But that was part of a future that none of us could contemplate quite yet.

Bob and I drove the Thelans and Tom to the airport for their flight while Brad went to be with friends. I still wasn't ready to part with these wonderful people. At Boston's Logan Airport terminal, we hugged and renewed the promise to stay in touch. It was hard to see them go, and I tearfully hugged Maureen and Laura an extra time. Bob and I watched them disappear into the US Airways crowd and climbed back into the SUV to head home, alone for the first time in a week.

We drove home in near silence; I wish we could have comforted each other, but we were in too much pain to even listen to music. Bob was driving, and occasionally, I'd notice him unconsciously shaking his head silently in what looked like disbelief. We spent that evening at home in near darkness, too devastated to watch TV or read. I couldn't concentrate on anything; nothing sank in. When I tried to listen to music, it made me feel worse. But the full reality wouldn't hit us until the next day.

REFLECTION:

What can be worse than burying your child? No wonder we were operating in a fog with a numbness, which partly protected us. Only short-term tasks and deadlines forced us to keep moving. We were no longer in <u>denial,</u> of course, about Brent's death, but we were blessedly unaware of the impact it would have on us. We were still <u>bargaining</u> for Brad's safety and Brent's spirit. We were beginning to feel more surges of <u>anger,</u> wondering, "Why us?" The early stages of <u>depression</u> were starting to appear for each of us. <u>Acceptance</u> was inevitable, of course. What we had not <u>accepted</u> yet was our life going forward without Brent. We were moving between the stages of grief, and we had no clue how much worse it was going to get.

Everything took on a greater significance for me. I was still upset at the efforts by our local priests to fit the funeral into some preconceived, off-the-shelf idea about what a funeral needed to be like. In those moments of tremendous loss, their need to stick with procedures seemed callous. For us, Brent's last ceremony on earth needed to be very personal and unique to him. It is inconceivable that anyone would interfere with the way in which a parent wants to put their child to rest. It was obvious they'd never been through it—one of many reasons I feel that priests should be allowed to marry, have kids and real-world experiences before trying to counsel others.

Life certainly has a way of moving on regardless of what we're going through. You could find no greater illustration of that than having Brad's high school graduation scheduled in the same week as his brother's wake and funeral. With the help of family and friends, we got through it.

We were fortunate that we had an army of people around us, caring about us, feeding us, trying to help us in any way they could. Unfortunately, not everyone has that luxury. They helped tremendously, but no one could help with the most painful decisions. That can be very lonely especially in situations where a single parent needs to deal with it on their own.

I think it is common to idealize children that die, like they have no faults. I'm sure we did that ourselves, but I remember trying not to overdo it. We all have faults, even Brent. When we put the lost child on an unrealistic pedestal, it makes it harder for those remaining. They could never live up to their sibling's memory; they may even resent them.

Also, if there is only one child remaining, as in Brad's case, he or she must feel very alone too. They've lost their sibling, the only one in the immediate family with whom they've shared experiences, a generation, and perhaps an occasional conspiracy.

When a sibling loses a twin, it must be especially difficult, like losing a big part of themselves. There is an entire range of emotions that uniquely reflect how we experience the loss of a child, grandchild, or sibling depending on timing, ages, locations, relationships, and family dynamics—even depending on the cause of death. Grieving is very complicated, with many layers. In the end, though, one thing is common to that experience: we all need help. That help can come in many forms; but initially, the kind of help that seems most useful allows us to acknowledge our loss, experience it, and help with whatever needs doing.

I believe it is important not to avoid those in grief. People worry that they might say something that will cause more pain. To those of us experiencing the loss, it usually doesn't have that effect; instead, it brings acknowledgement and comfort. Overwhelmingly, what I hear from the bereaved families in the support group I run is that they want people to offer condolences. No one can cause them more pain than they are already in. You can't remind them of something they never forget. The loss of a child feels fresh for a very long time. Mentioning him or her does not bring the pain to the surface; it is already there. It does, however, honor the child's memory.

So if you can manage it, offer condolences and be willing to listen. Let us vent. We need to express our feelings, and it can be difficult to find someone willing to listen. I remember talking about my loss to anyone who'd listen, whether strangers or not. Sometimes they'd get wide-eyed and slip away as fast as they could. I wondered if they thought my loss was contagious.

Part 2
Reflecting Back

Chapter 7
A Child's Death Rocks Your World

SO FAR, I'VE shared in detail my experience of losing Brent and the emotions I felt during the weeks after his death. I've tried to impart what I've come to know as some of the feelings that I believe most parents are likely to experience when moving through the loss of a child.

But from this point forward, I think it might be more useful looking at those experiences with the gift of hindsight after having begun a healing journey and having worked with other families who have lost children.

I'd also like to reflect briefly on my two other losses: a miscarriage and a stillbirth. The emotional impact of these experiences remained dormant for a long time, but eventually, the methods of healing I learned after Brent's death allowed me to work through the feelings from those earlier losses too.

The grief of Brent's death brought back the heartache of losing his brother, Robbie, stillborn fifteen years earlier. In my response to Brent's death, the grief associated with Robbie's death took on a surprising sense of immediacy, almost as if it had just happened. And it released the grief I'd perhaps buried following my first miscarriage.

A recent death often stirs up old grief, especially if you haven't really reconciled with those earlier losses. Apparently, I hadn't.

Six years after Bob and I were married, at the age of twenty-seven, I experienced both the fear and delight that accompanies a first pregnancy. Elated, I sensed that my life was changing forever. Excitedly, we informed family and friends of the pregnancy, and they shared in our happiness. But at the end of my first trimester, I began spotting and finally lost the baby. We were heartbroken; it was my first real encounter with grief other than that associated with the loss of a grandparent.

Looking back, I realize that my grief was somewhat tempered by the fact that I hadn't yet experienced the joys and sorrows, the fun and hard work of raising a child. I didn't really know what I had missed, but as a result of this loss, Bob and I became closer and sought comfort from each other as we tried to heal.

Miscarriages often happen; we knew that. It had happened to my parents, my older sister, my husband's parents, and some of our friends. Still, it hurt, and the hurt took a while to heal.

A few years later, I had a normal healthy pregnancy and gave birth to Brent, who was both perfectly formed and a challenge from the start. Two years after he was born, I had another full-term normal pregnancy and gave birth to Brad. By then, I was nearly age thirty-one. Brad too was a perfectly healthy child and, in terms of parenting, a challenge in his own unique way. It amazed me that brothers could be so different.

Brent was extroverted, talkative, and hyper while Brad was introverted, quiet, and determined. They resembled each other physically but had very different personalities, styles, and even body types. It was apparent Brad would soon outsize his older brother.

Throughout their infancies and childhoods, I discovered that I loved being a mother. I bonded so strongly with them that I still find the depth of the experience difficult to describe.

We settled into our family life, which I loved, although I was also busy at work and traveling on business. We didn't plan to have any more children. But a few years later, when Brent was six and Brad four, I found myself pregnant again. I understood the drill by now and took good care of myself. I was very comfortable with my pregnancy. After all, I'd had two healthy pregnancies with natural childbirth, and I expected no problems.

My two older boys were born in New Jersey. But by the time I was pregnant with Robbie, we had moved to Massachusetts where I chose an obstetrician in private practice. I went for regular visits with my new doctor. Everything seemed fine, although the doctor told us he was having trouble hearing a strong heartbeat. Nevertheless, he continued to assure us it was nothing to worry about. I believed him because I could feel the baby moving, although I noticed it was not as active as the boys had been. Still, I didn't worry about it. I didn't know if a girl might be less active, or maybe I was just experiencing this pregnancy differently. Everything changed suddenly during my six-month checkup.

By midterm in my pregnancy, my doctor had merged with an OB-GYN group in a nearby town. They rotated staff doctors with all their pregnant patients, so each doctor would be familiar with each patient in case any of them were on call for the delivery. During this particular checkup, another doctor performed a standard ultrasound. That test confirmed my doctor's concern about not hearing a strong heartbeat, but what she found shocked us. This obstetrician, new to us, invited us into her office and gently informed us that our unborn baby had serious problems; that (s)he would probably not survive.

I couldn't believe what I was hearing. The world seemed to stop. I felt like I was being spoken to in a foreign language. In a voice I could barely recognize, I heard myself ask, "'What's wrong?"

I glanced at Bob; his face was stricken, so I reached for his hand and held on tight.

"Your baby has only one chamber in his heart instead of the normal four. He's missing one of his kidneys, and his liver is in the wrong place."

My hands and feet went cold. "Oh my God," I mumbled.

She went on to explain that the baby also had a cleft palate, shortened forearms, and possibly other issues. I stared at her, trying to come to terms with the terrible news she'd just delivered.

The doctor said that they had scheduled an appointment with a specialist in Boston to confirm the diagnosis. She advised us to terminate the pregnancy because, she said, the baby would not survive to full term. It was clear to her that even if (s)he did, (s)he would not survive childbirth. And, if by some miracle the baby did that, many surgeries would be necessary to keep him or her alive. In any case, our baby would not have a normal, functional life.

Bob and I sat there in shock. He was silent; I was

crying, but I started to feel a protective numbness setting in.

"Why?" Bob asked. "What caused this?"

She shook her head. "We don't know," she said. "We may never know. I'm so very sorry,".

Yes, me too, I thought.

Bob and I experienced a long, restless night talking and crying quietly in each other's arms, trying not to let the boys hear. We prayed that this doctor was wrong, that there might be a way to improve the situation and save the baby.

The next morning, sad and tired, we headed into Boston to see the specialist, a physician whose practice was devoted to problematic pregnancies. She seemed sensitive to our feelings and appeared to be competent. She performed additional tests and a more extensive and precise ultrasound. As she did this, she pointed out several problems confirming what the local doctor had told us as well as finding some additional issues.

She told us the cause was a genetic malfunction during conception, a "syndrome" with a name I can no longer remember. It happened only once in a million pregnancies, she said, and was very unlikely to happen to us a second time should we decide to have another child.

I remember thinking that I was thirty-five, this pregnancy was unplanned, I had two healthy sons, and even if there was only a tiny chance of this sort of thing happening again, I didn't want to take that chance. After fourteen years of marriage, Bob and I were experiencing a few problems, and I'd hoped this baby would help fix that and bring us closer again.

At this point, we didn't know the baby's gender, nor

had we chosen a name. But when the doctor asked if we wanted to know the gender, we replied yes. She said that I was carrying a baby boy. Hearing this made the infant seem even more real to us.

When we'd considered boys' names before, we hadn't named our sons after Bob to avoid the nickname Junior. But now, we decided to name this baby Robert Francis, after his father and grandparents. Bob's father was Francis, his mother was Frances and my father's middle name was Francis. We would call him Robbie.

We asked the specialist about our options and told her that our local obstetrician had advised us to terminate. This doctor looked puzzled then explained that in our case, this discovery was made too late; we were one week past the legal cutoff in Massachusetts.

I felt a surge of anger so strong that it shocked me! I was already sad and hurt, and now I was furious. I felt like "they" were making life decisions about my body and my family that they had no right to make. I had not had time to absorb all this, never mind decide anything. As we drove home from Boston, I was still angry that my primary obstetrician hadn't found the problems earlier. We may still have been faced with a horrible situation, but we could have had options. Anger, sadness, and even the earliest stages of grief were all churning inside me.

That evening, we went back to our local obstetric office and spoke with one of the practice's founding doctors. He expressed sympathy and concern and said they were working on alternatives for us. Although this felt like they cared superficially, I couldn't help wondering if they were just protecting themselves, afraid we might file a lawsuit. The next day, we got a call from Dr. Joe, another doctor in the group. He seemed more genuinely concerned. Somehow he'd found two alternative clinics in nearby states where we could have the pregnancy terminated. He offered to make the arrangements if that was what we wanted. Now we really did have to choose. It felt like the toughest decision of my life.

I was a wreck; I did not go to work for three days. Visibly pregnant with Robbie, I was more aware now of his lack of movement. I felt grief-stricken. A decision had to be made quickly.

We agonized for those three horrible days. We'd never before discussed abortion as a choice, and I'm not sure that we had strong views in either direction. We discussed the issue with Dr. Joe and my sister, a nurse, as well as with friends and family. We even met with my sister's boss, a medical doctor and family practice owner who had offered to help us talk through making the decision.

We considered the moral and religious aspects of termination, the baby's quality of life if he were to live, the impact on Brent and Brad, and the likelihood that we could be choosing a difficult life of hospitals, surgeries, and tough recoveries. We also considered what it would be like to continue the pregnancy. Soon we'd both have to return to work and get on with our lives. I would be responding to well-meaning questions about the impending birth. Either choice would be difficult at best.

Bob felt badly about either alternative, but since I was carrying the baby and would endure most of the immediate challenges, he said that he would support whatever I decided.

In the end, I kept returning to the story I'd been told about my own birth. The doctors had informed my mother that giving birth to me would kill her. She'd had tuberculosis, which had left her in a weakened condition. They advised her to terminate the pregnancy. Her doctors believed that childbirth and early infant care would be dangerous for her, possibly fatal. A devout Catholic, she refused to end the pregnancy; instead she went home to Maine to get help from her mother and sisters.

Shortly after she made that trip, I was born two months premature. Although I struggled in an incubator for a few weeks, I soon began to thrive. My mother survived too, and somehow, the pregnancy seemed to resolve some of her medical issues that doctors had been trying to treat for years. They called it a miracle and had been wrong about her pregnancy.

After much soul-searching, I decided to continue my pregnancy and deal with whatever arose. I was already emotionally attached to Robbie. I had to give my baby every chance to prove these doctors wrong!

The next several weeks were very difficult. We chose not to tell the boys since they were too young to understand, and we didn't really know the outcome. When they asked, we did tell them I was carrying a boy. It was painful seeing them excited about the idea of having a little brother. We couldn't show our real feelings to them. I remember going to work every day looking very pregnant and having people ask me when I was due and how I felt. Not fun.

This continued for approximately six more weeks, during which I had weekly checkups. In my eighth month, just before Thanksgiving and after we'd moved to the new home we'd built in Newburyport, Massachusetts, doctors found no heartbeat. After performing a blood test, they informed us that Robbie had died in utero. So they had been right after all. But I was okay with the path

I'd chosen. I supposed this was similar in some ways to having a terminally ill child, except I hadn't gotten to know or rear Robbie, nor had I suffered with him through a long illness.

Now I was left with two choices. I could wait and let my body reject the baby in its own time or let the doctors induce birth with Pitocin. I couldn't bear spending an unknown number of days with Robbie dead inside me. I needed to deliver him, meet him, say good-bye to him, bury him, and start moving through my grief so that we could move on with our lives. I also wanted to give birth before Thanksgiving, so I could spend the holiday weekend with family for support. Secretly, I was afraid Robbie might start to decompose inside me, and I couldn't take that chance.

Later that day, I was admitted to the obstetrics department at the local hospital. It was heart-wrenching, listening to the other mothers experiencing normal childbirth, hearing crying babies, seeing happy new parents. The staff hooked me up to an IV to start the Pitocin. I'd had relatively short labors and natural childbirths with Brent and Brad, but this labor lasted for two and a half days of intermittent pain and exhaustion.

Bob was there as much as he could be, but he was caring for the boys with help from my mother and sister. Finally, on the third day, I went into hard labor that was much worse than I'd experienced with my other boys; perhaps because the baby wasn't able to help. All of this was compounded by my emotional pain and the stress of the circumstances.

Robert Francis DeLibero was born and officially died on November 20th, coincidentally a Friday; his two brothers were also born on Fridays. The nurses took him out of sight, cleaned him, and brought him back to Bob and me, wrapped tightly in a light blue baby blanket.

The nurse had tears in her eyes and mumbled that she was sorry when she handed Robbie to Bob. It was so very sad to see. Robbie's eyes were closed, and he had a small triangular mouth caused by his cleft palate. But otherwise, he looked just like Brent and Brad when they were born—all three so similar to each other, so adorable and unmistakably brothers. Even with Robbie's medical challenges, he was only three inches shorter than his brothers had been at birth, but he was half their weight.

Bob had always been great with the boys when they were babies. He seemed so attuned to them at that stage in their lives—more natural at it than I was. I was better with them in later stages. Bob was very close to his sons; he probably saw them as an extension of himself. The sense of pain and loss was visible on his face while he held Robbie, inhaled the baby's scent, kissed his forehead, peeked inside his blanket, but did not unwrap him. He seemed afraid that he might disturb his little son.

When it was my turn to hold Robbie, I felt so much love and such a strong connection to him. I was so sorry that I'd never get to know him. And I was sad that he and his brothers would never know each other. I understood that it would have been a tough life for him and for us. We'd been willing to take it on, and it was hard to hold him knowing we would never get that chance.

When the nurse came to take Robbie away, it felt like she was literally ripping off a piece of me, a piece that I knew I'd never get back. Part of me, part of our family, was gone forever.

Bob told me much later that he would always have

strong memories of those moments when he'd held Robbie. He was moved by Robbie's close resemblance to Brent and Brad. Bob remembered the "baby smell" of him, and said he could have held him for hours. He was heartbroken and felt sad that Robbie had to struggle to survive as long as he had.

We did not take a picture of Robbie; in hindsight, I wish we had. At the time, I didn't want to remember him as disfigured; I couldn't even bear to look under the blanket to see if he really had been born with shortened forearms. Back then, hospitals did not take pictures of stillborn infants like they do now, and so it felt morbid to ask.

They gave us a little card bearing his name, birth date, and an ink imprint of his tiny feet with a booklet containing poems that related to the loss of an infant. I still have it twenty-five years later. I vividly remember how difficult it was to let them take him away as we broke down and wept.

After they took Robbie from my arms, I couldn't get out of there soon enough. I asked the staff, who seemed to understand, to move me out of the birthing center. They did. But by the time I was settled in a new hospital room, I wanted to get out of the hospital altogether. Emotionally, I was a mess; physically, I was fine. When yet another doctor came to check on me, I told him I felt all right and asked him if I might be released that day. He just said he was sorry and he'd check back later on that evening to see how I was doing.

"I'm leaving today, even if I have to sign myself out," I said. The look on his face told me he didn't care for this comment.

"I'm fine physically. I need to get out of this environment, away from all the new mothers, babies, and the place where I lost Robbie," I said.

I added that we had plans to drive to New Jersey that weekend to be with family on Thanksgiving. He gave me a strange look and said he'd be back, but I knew he wasn't happy. I tried sleeping, with little success, managing only a short nap. I was exhausted on so many levels and so very, very sad. By then, the realization had set in that we needed to break the bad news to our other sons.

I asked my mother and sister to call the local church and funeral director. They arranged for a simple white stone casket along with a simple graveside service the next morning. The cemetery representative told them we could bury Robbie in the same plot with my father, who had died three years earlier; my mother's future plot was allocated beside him. At least Robbie would be with his grandparents. I believed my father would look after Robbie for us.

I could think only about getting out of the hospital and going home. I wanted to see Brent and Brad and hug them. Knowing that they had lost their little brother made me appreciate them even more, and I dreaded having to tell them about Robbie.

The doctor finally came back, examined me, and agreed to let me go home that night, but he warned me to take it easy.

Leaving that environment helped a little. I wanted to feel happy for the other mothers but couldn't yet—not when I had to leave without my baby. But I thought it would help to focus on my family—on what we needed to function, grieve, and heal.

Bob brought me home; the boys were still up when we

got there. My mother was with them. I was so happy to see them and hugged them each tightly, trying not to let them see me cry. But even at ages four and six, they seemed to sense my sadness.

"What's wrong, Mommy, are you OK?" This and other questions were mostly from our gregarious six-year-old Brent. Brad let his older brother do most of his talking while he stood right beside him, eager to hear the answers.

We went into the living room and sat on the couch. Bob and I each held one of the boys in our laps; Nana sat in a chair nearby.

"We have to explain some things," Bob said.

They were so adorable, all ready for bed with that nice after-bath smell and wearing their brightly colored Winnie-the-Pooh pajamas with feet. I wanted things to stay like that forever. I so wished I was holding a healthy Robbie so they could meet him.

It was hard to start, so we talked about what they'd been doing while I was in the hospital over the last three days. They excitedly told me about playtime, school, and friends as well as puzzles they'd been working on with Nana, who loved puzzles.

"Where's the baby?" Brent finally asked.

They seemed thrilled at the thought of having a new playmate, someone to chase, wrestle with, and play tricks on. Brent had already been a big brother, and he may have remembered what it was like when Brad was a new baby. I think Brad was looking forward to being a big brother.

How do you explain to two little boys that their brother has died even before they could meet him? I wanted to be truthful, but I also wanted to minimize the hurt, and I did not want to scare them. Finally, I couldn't avoid it any longer.

"Well, you have a little brother whose name is Robbie," I said. "But something went wrong while he was being born, and he had to go to heaven. He won't be coming home."

My heart broke as their expressions changed from smiles to frowns and then to saddened bewilderment. They didn't understand; how could they? I didn't want them thinking it could happen to them or worrying that Robbie was alone and afraid.

Bob tried to help them. "Hey guys, you do have a little brother, but he's gone to live with God and Pop and Grandma. Pop and Grandma will watch over him. Do you remember your grandparents?"

With sad faces, they nodded slowly. Whereas my father had died three years earlier when they were too little then to understand fully; Bob's mother died just a year ago They remembered her.

"Robbie won't be coming home," Bob continued. "He's an angel in heaven now. But he looks a lot like you guys when you were babies, and he loves you very much. We love him too, and we're going to have a service tomorrow morning to say good-bye to him. You guys are coming with us, OK,and the day after that, we're going to drive to New Jersey to spend Thanksgiving with your cousins and Aunt Rita and Uncle Joe's family. Nana will be with us."

They nodded. Tears were rolling down their cheeks as they asked a few questions to better understand what he was like, and why their little brother wasn't coming home. They already missed Robbie even though they had never met him. We tried to answer as simply as we could and repeatedly hugged them. I tried but couldn't stop my tears. We reassured them that we missed Robbie too, but we were okay. We might be sad for a while, of course, but it wasn't because of them, and we would all feel better in time. We told our boys that we felt so blessed to have them and how much we loved them. Then we explained we'd include Robbie in their nightly prayers, and he'd look down on us—our own little angel in heaven.

We tucked them into bed with extra hugs and kisses and went to bed ourselves, exhausted. What a day it had been; I'd started out the morning in the hospital, delivered my third son, experienced his birth and his death in the same day, came home against doctor's orders, and tried to explain all this to my other children. I did not sleep well, thinking about Robbie, and woke up crying during the night. It would be a hard week ahead. We had to face telling family and friends, to bury Robbie, and then try to celebrate Thanksgiving.

The next morning was unseasonably cold for November, even in New England. We bundled ourselves and the boys up and headed over to St. Mary's Cemetery to meet Father Bob, the pastor. Even through heavy coats, hats, and gloves, we felt the bitter cold.

"This is how it should be when you bury someone," Bob said. "Somehow the cold makes sense."

A small white carved-stone box, approximately one foot wide and deep by two feet long, held Robbie's little body wrapped in blankets. It sat on the cold ground next to my father's plot. The cemetery staff would lower it into the ground after we left. There was no formal ceremony, just a simple reading, some prayers, and a blessing by the priest. Robbie had been baptized and given last rites after his birth at the hospital. Only a few members of the immediate family attended the short memorial. The boys didn't fully understand, but they seemed to know they were praying for and saying good-bye to their little brother. The adults were tearful yet mindful of the need to comfort our kids.

We considered not taking the boys to the service but felt they should have an opportunity to say good-bye. We thought that it might be important to allow them to grieve their loss as well, despite their tender age. My parents always brought me to wakes and funerals as a child; it was considered a sad but normal part of life.

When the short service was finished, we thanked the priest and said one last good-bye to Robbie, each of us laying a hand on the tiny cold casket. Then we headed home with our family for hot coffee and a warm breakfast.

Talking through the experience was helpful. We needed to grieve Robbie's loss even though he hadn't survived one day of life. I believe this is true for other parents who experience a stillborn child, or one who lives only a very short time.

Immediate and extended family and close friends were supportive, but I was surprised that few others offered help, condolences, or sent cards even though from our point of view, we'd experienced our infant's passing as we would any other death. Others did not seem to understand the depth of our pain and grief. It was almost like Robbie had not been a real person in their eyes; like his death somehow did not count or hurt as much as if he'd been an older child.

I took a few days off to heal after his birth, but it had really been more of an emotional than a physical ordeal for me. There were no stitches to recover from, just a broken heart.

But I had retained as much extra weight carrying Robbie as I had with his brothers. Like any mother after childbirth, I had all the usual struggles working hard to lose weight. However, I didn't have the joy of a new baby to make the struggle worthwhile; it felt very unfair.

We drove home the Sunday after Thanksgiving and tried to get back into normal routines, but it wasn't easy. Both boys, but especially Brent, would occasionally ask about Robbie, and they included him in their nightly prayers. Brent even asked to go to the cemetery a few times to visit Robbie and his grandfather, which I found touching because he was only seven. The visit to the grave seemed to make him feel better. In nicer weather, we'd stay a while with Robbie and Pop, talk about them, and leave flowers behind. Their grandmother was interned in New Jersey.

Bob and I busied ourselves in work. We still had to deal with all the tasks related to our new house and getting ready for Christmas. Bob started a new family tradition of making a homemade pine blanket from extra branches trimmed off our Christmas tree. The boys and I would then help decorate it, and we'd go together to lay it on Robbie's grave. We visited his gravesite often at first, but that eventually tapered off to significant days like the anniversary of his birth/death and Christmas.

After Brent died fifteen years later, I found many of the old feelings of grief I experienced with Robbie resurfacing, but even more intensely. Maybe I hadn't finished grieving Robbie at the time.

My mother died after Robbie and before Brent; so my mother, father, and Robbie were buried in one place and

Brent in another part of the same cemetery. We visited them all more often after Brent's death and now made two Christmas wreaths or blankets, one for each grave.

THE IMPACT OF LOSING BRENT

It's difficult to describe just how completely the loss of a child rocks your world. Stress levels are very high; my world not only changed, but as it turned out, my marriage and even my life were at risk. While all changes bring challenges, the death of a child is particularly traumatic. It is permanent, and it requires a tremendous amount of work, healing, and the passage of time to enable you to find a "new normal." But it will happen.

Every family and every family member is unique in how they experience and then deal with this enormous change. With my family, even within the same household, each of us felt the impact of Brent's death in so many unique ways. We reacted, grieved, and coped differently. For example, I reached out to others to help me heal. Bob went inward and did a lot of writing. Brad got even more quiet and resisted outside help. Those very differences added to the complexity of our grief as we found each other behaving very differently than expected. I now realize that this is part of the process. Recovery requires a significant amount of patience, tolerance for others, and a commitment to self-care. What made it worse for me is that all of this happened while I was questioning everything in my world. I was also trying to reconcile myself to a reality that goes against deeply held beliefs: that I *should be able to protect my children; they are not supposed to die before me.*

Metaphorically, I felt that I didn't have any will or strength; one day I just hit a wall, collapsed in a heap at the base of that wall, and lost any sense of forward momentum in my life. I had no strength, no desire to go on. I could not see my way around this enormous wall.

I'd never have guessed the immense impact on my life that first year following Brent's death. Parents that I talk with sometimes say they are numb that first year following their loss; that the second year is the worst. For me, the first year was definitely the worst. I struggled to function normally. I found it difficult to get out of bed in the morning. Making myself do simple chores around the house was hard, but it was even harder to make myself get dressed and leave the house. I found it impossible to read or focus my mind on anything for long. Going back to work and trying to be effective was a major challenge. I remember not being able to listen to music for at least three months. Everything reminded me of my loss. Nothing mattered anymore; nothing was of consequence. At the time, I didn't recognize these symptoms were a manifestation of depression.

I worried about the impact of Brent's death on my family, and I became desperate to get some confirmation that his spirit lived on. I was obsessed with the need to "memorialize" Brent, to make sure that his memory and life were celebrated and honored. In retrospect, I recognize that I was investing an unnatural level of energy and attention to the little things that remained of him: his pictures, his recorded voice, his possessions, his room—anything that related to him. And finally, there was a constant sense of fear and anxiety about the future and how the course of our lives might yet be altered. The first year, for me, was a mixture of profound experiences of the heart and spirit accompanied by significant changes in our day-to-day lives.

During this year, I was nearly laid off, partly a result of the grief and depression I was in. Ultimately, I changed jobs in IBM, then watched Brad struggle and flunk out of his first year of college. My marriage of thirty years faltered and finally ended, also in part because of the trauma we'd gone through and the differences in the way we dealt with it. At the worst possible juncture, I was also forced to live alone for the first time in my life.

Before Brent died, I had been preparing for a future that seemed clearly defined to me: a long-term, stable relationship, a comfortable retirement, and grandchildren. By year's end, all of that was in jeopardy. It was during this period—also a time of unexpected and significant financial stress brought on by these changes—that I found myself, at the age of fifty-one, having to start over.

And yet despite these changes, challenges, and struggles, some deep and ultimately sustaining things began to happen. I began a spiritual journey that greatly benefited me and still continues today. I'll explain more about that in the next chapter.

The tremendous support I received from family and friends was wonderful, and for a time, Bob and I seemed to get closer. I was able to channel the compulsion to memorialize Brent into helping others. Intuitively, I sensed that helping others would also help me. In addition, I gained some key spiritual insights that I might not have realized if I'd not been forced through this traumatic experience.

For example, it became crystal clear to me what was important in life and what was not. This seemingly simple insight gave me the freedom to choose not to put up with unimportant and negative things. I was then empowered to base decisions on what was important to me rather than making decisions based on what was important to others. For the first time in my life, I came to understand a spiritual connection between human beings and the universe, which went beyond any specific religious practice or orientation. This realization changed many of the beliefs I held earlier in my life, especially many of those dictated by my Catholic religion. This includes man-made doctrine and things like reincarnation.

Our lives continued. But that day after Brent's funeral, in many ways, the first without Brent, without an immediate purpose *and* without the supportive presence of so many friends and family was extremely difficult. After tossing and turning most of the night, I finally stopped trying to sleep. The difference that first morning was that I felt that I had no reason to get out of bed. With the wake and funeral behind us, there was nothing pressing to do, no decisions, no places any of us had to be. Brent was dead and buried. It was over. Even though Bob and I had each other and Brad, the reality of Brent's absence was setting in. It is hard to describe what I felt that morning, but my depression was deep.

The entire core of my body felt like it had been ripped out, gutted like a fish. Shaking, I curled up in a fetal position, turned away from Bob, tried to hold myself together with tears streaming down my face. Nothing seemed to ease my grief. I had no interest in eating or showering or doing anything.

Finally, I was able to compose myself enough to turn over and look at Bob. He lay quietly on his back, his eyes open, and his cheeks wet. He looked dazed. I reached out to him, and we hugged and wept together. When I tried to ask him how he was doing, my voice sounded hollow, distant. He just shook his head and sobbed. He looked irretrievably lost.

That week, I became deeply worried about him. I had to take him to the doctor; his blood pressure had spiked so high that he was stumbling and slurring his words. They temporarily medicated him to ease his anxiety and bring his blood pressure down. There was nothing, however, they could prescribe for his broken heart.

When I think back on those first weeks after Brent's funeral, the word *zombie* seems most appropriate. I felt as if I'd suddenly become profoundly stupid and unfocused. Detached, barely engaged, I found it hard to watch, read, or listen. I am not a nap taker, but now I took a lot of short naps, usually crying myself to sleep. I looked at every sympathy card over and over; they seemed to arrive daily for weeks. We were surprised to find some from people we didn't know and from other bereaved parents who'd read Brent's obituary in the newspaper. Their wonderful comforting notes were sometimes accompanied by books about grief. We received countless phone calls and visits filled with kind wishes from friends, family, and acquaintances; some of them brought food for us. I walked a lot on the beach with some of those friends. Still, in those first weeks, I was just surviving one day, one hour, one minute at a time. I dressed very casually—no makeup, nothing fancy, nothing that required much thought or effort.

Bob seemed to act similar to how I was feeling, not his usual self; it was an effort to accomplish anything. He dressed only for comfort. I could see the pain he was enduring. What a delicate state he was in that week. We needed each other; we spent a lot of time sitting and talking about Brent.

This was our pattern for a while—a new experience for us. The only thing that made sense and got our attention was the overwhelming pain. Even when we could manage a good moment, such as laughing at something on TV or being invited to a party, it didn't last. Nights were the worst—endless hours without sleep, merely dozing, alternating between brooding and crying. Lovemaking was much less frequent and sometimes initiated from trying to comfort each other's grief through physical closeness.

Brad stayed in his room and was very quiet. Sometimes, he would go out with his friends, or they would spend time with him at the house, nearly always in his room. I was glad they were there for him. To this day, he doesn't reach out much. We'd try to engage him in conversation to check on how he was doing; I'm sure he was equally worried about how we were doing. It had to be hard for him not to have his brother to share his feelings with.

After the first week, Brad decided that he wanted to get a tattoo to honor Brent, but he didn't mention it. He and three friends piled into our Ford Explorer and drove across the state border into Seabrook, New Hampshire, headed for a tattoo parlor. A short while later, he called to tell us he had been in a car accident.

My reaction was raw emotion; I heard myself screaming, "No!" Finally, I was able to hear him assure me that he and his friends were all right, and I calmed down. Although I realized that he was calling me and therefore not in grave danger, fear for my remaining child filled me—seemed possess me. Today, I understand that commonly hap after you've lost a child; you are more afraid for your other children's safety.

When we finally saw the truck, we were amazed that no one had been seriously hurt, just a little scraped up from the deployment of the air bags. I experienced a range of emotions. I was grateful that no one was hurt, but angry at Brad for not wearing seat belts and angry at Brent for somehow not protecting his brother. Clearly, there was little logic to my response. Thinking about it later, I came to believe that maybe Brent had helped; their injuries could have been much worse.

Believing that Brent was still engaged on some level, still able to act on behalf of those he loved, became a source a great comfort to me. While the accident didn't lessen my irrational urge to keep Brad in a protective bubble, it did allow me to cope with that accident and understand that it could turn out all right.

In many ways, the emotional roller coaster seemed to gather speed that first year. Fairly ordinary things would take on greater importance and provoke powerful emotional responses in me. I remember when the death certificate arrived, it was dated May 31, the day the doctors pronounced Brent "brain-dead." This was deeply upsetting to me; I felt that it ignored the last day we spent with Brent. Our hands had been on his heart when it stopped

‌ting; it was June 1 when I'd felt his spirit leave and the

ᵔ cold. I could not let them deny us the last day

ᵈ even if the doctors had already pronounced

It became my mission to get the date on

ᵔ changed to reflect our experience

ᵎy intense emotional state, I found

ᵔ whoever was on the other end of the

phone then dissolving into sobs as I attempted to explain why I wanted the date changed.

We bereaved parents find ourselves clinging to anything that evokes the memory of our child. In those early days, we become very protective of their memory as we come to grips with the reality that we can no longer protect them from physical harm.

Hearing Brent's voice on the answering machine took on increased importance to us. Bob and I often caught each other replaying it. Like so much of what we were experiencing, it was both painful and wonderful to hear Brent, and these emotions would alternate with lightning speed. We were so grateful to have his voice, but sad at this reminder that he was gone. Bob copied it into a tape recorder multiple times to safeguard it. We were afraid that we might forget the sound of his voice, and were horrified by that thought. Even years later, when a phone repair person deleted it accidentally, I was devastated.

Photographs, which we took of Brent, also gained importance. I searched for and developed the pictures from a disposable camera I'd used when we'd been in Arizona for Brent's twenty-first birthday. It held shots of all of us, including Laura, and were the last we'd taken with him. When the pictures were returned, they were cloudy, barely discernible, damaged from accidental X-ray screening. This was yet another incident that caused me great anguish. I became obsessed with making those photos clear. I brought the negatives and prints to several photo shops until I finally found one that could increase the clarity of the picture until it was acceptable. I was already kicking myself for forgetting to bring my digital camera to his birthday celebration and for succumbing to his pressure not to take as many pictures as I usually did when we were together. These little things mean a lot when the little things are all that remain.

The videotape from the memorial service was another thing we became very grateful for. Alan gave us six copies to share with family members even before we'd realized how important those tapes would be for years to come. When we felt we could endure it, Bob, Brad. and I sat and watched it together. We listened to our friends and family share their love for Brent with affection and humor, which meant a great deal to us. I later used that tape to introduce Brent to people in my life who never had a chance to meet him; I still do; it really portrays who he was.

After only two weeks, I attempted my return to work. In hindsight, I realize that it was too soon. My boss and colleagues at IBM were very supportive, but I was in a high-stress consulting and sales job with the constant pressure of quotas, customer relationship, profitability, and team management responsibilities. Before we lost Brent, I'd already decided I wanted to change jobs within IBM but had not been able to get approval from my vice president. After this tragedy, it became crystal clear to me what was important and what was not. In the new scheme of things, this job was in the "not" category. It was important to help support us financially, yes; but after the loss of my son, I was no longer willing to endure the stress of being miserable in my job.

Shortly after I returned to work, I explained to my manager that the worst thing that could possibly happen to me had happened. It had put things in perspective for me; I no longer feared anything that could happen to me at work, nor did I care any longer about deadlines and quotas.

I made it clear that he needed to let me look for another job within IBM or I'd have to leave the company. He finally agreed and started moving my customer accounts to my colleagues. Though I wasn't in a job-hunting mood, the transition gave me a little breathing room that I desperately needed. However, it ended up causing another kind of stress.

IBM Global Services was doing rounds of layoffs, and when my customers were given to someone else, I was unable to meet my quota, which put me at risk. Now we faced serious financial stress on top of deep grief, but just in time, I found another IBM position. My new boss was very compassionate, cut me some slack, and allowed me time to learn my new job. It was still hard to concentrate, but it was good to be doing something different: learning new areas with new people and less pressure.

In his grief, Bob decided not to continue working in auto sales. Just before Brent's accident, he'd accepted a promotion to the position of financial manager for the car dealership. A month or so after Brent's funeral, Bob took a week-long business trip for training to prepare for his new job responsibilities. He found it extremely sad and difficult to be away from home. To make matters worse, an incident upset him greatly while in Texas. He saw a front-page newspaper story with a picture of a father in a wheelchair, his child standing next to him with his hand on his father's shoulder. There were four caskets set in front of them. The father had fallen asleep at the wheel driving his family of six; his wife and three of his four children died in the resulting accident. Bob was deeply affected by this. It was a tough week for him, and he found it hard to concentrate on the training.

By the time he came home, he had already decided that he didn't want the promotion; shortly after that, he decided not to return to work. The idea of negotiating car prices and dealing with typical car shopper requests felt too inconsequential to him after the enormity of losing his son.

I understood. It was difficult to accept that the world could continue to function normally when you've lost a child; your world has ground to a halt, so why hasn't everyone else's? Bob resigned, but it took him a while to stabilize emotionally. For me, I needed to keep busy; I hoped it would help. Also, financially, now more than ever, we needed the income.

Less than six weeks after Brent died, I reached my fiftieth birthday. No one knew what to do for me; even I didn't know if or how I wanted to celebrate it. I'd already planned a fourth of July party at home and decided to go ahead with it. My family tried to turn that into a birthday party, but it didn't work well. I suppose everyone was reluctant to celebrate anything around me. Shortly afterward, my friend Julie, who seemed to understand, invited my family to dinner then had some close friends over as a surprise, so it was special. My emotions were causing me to be oversensitive, and I needed someone to do something just for me on my milestone birthday.

In trying to find ways to manage our grief, we had an emotional requirement to visit the cemetery daily. I did this regardless of the weather. Twice that first winter, my lightweight sporty car got stuck in snow, and I had to call a tow truck to pull me out before it grew dark and the gates of the cemetery closed. Despite their promise, the operators of the cemetery had not paved the section where Brent was buried; to this day, it remains a muddy and often barely passable road. But I'd go there in all kinds of weather, getting out of my car to touch Brent's grave and talk to him. Once, I stepped into deep snow that fell inside my boots, stinging my bare legs, but I hardly noticed.

Despite all of these challenges, I always found it beautiful and peaceful there. Everything was covered in fresh white snow painted by the fading light of dusk; the scene resonated with tranquility. The white landscape was broken intermittently by the salmon, gray, and black of the headstones, the colors of small American flags, and bright fake flowers or personal memorabilia. Somehow, it seemed quieter when it snowed—the cemetery an oasis among the surrounding houses, stores and busy streets.

Once, just before I was due on a mandatory conference call with my boss, my car became stuck in snow and ice, and I was forced to take the call on my cell phone, right there in the cemetery. The IBM executives and salespeople had no idea where I was, and I wasn't inclined to tell them. What would I have said? "Excuse me, I'm stuck in a graveyard. It's cold and getting dark, any ideas?"

I tried to focus on the call, thankful that technology allowed me to take calls from just about anywhere. I put the phone on speaker and muted it then carefully laid it on the seat beside me, trying to listen to the conversation while I tried to free the car by using the manual transmission to rock it out of mud and snow. No luck.

As the IBM teams reviewed sales deals in each geographical territory, I kept rocking the car and tried listening for prospects in my focus industries while hoping my boss wouldn't call on me to participate more actively. Then I grabbed my phone, held it to my ear, got out and looked for anything to put under the tires for traction; again, no luck. Back in the car with freezing feet and wet shoes, I heard the rest of the call while rubbing my hands together to warm up. How the hell would I get out of there?

At the end of the call, one of my peers—Jim, a salesperson from California—asked me to stay on the phone. He'd noticed that I was unusually quiet and asked what was wrong. Feeling a little silly, I explained the situation.

"Why don't you call AAA?" he asked.

We laughed at the absurdity of my not having come up with this obvious solution. As sad and stupid as I felt, I was also relieved, but this was another example of not thinking clearly in my grief. A short time later and after dark, a tow truck arrived, and I was on my way.

During that first winter, I started to talk to other bereaved parents in my area to figure out how I could help. The universe seemed to connect me with those who needed this kind of support. I became hyper aware of local children's deaths from the newspaper and was referred by friends, either to people who wanted help or to people who wanted to help us. I would also randomly meet bereaved parents in many situations—too often for coincidence, and somehow we'd know within a few minutes.

I'm very grateful for all those that helped, donated, and participated because we all helped each other—we still do. They're too many to mention, and name all their children that have passed on, here, but they are all in my thoughts and prayers. Maria helped me start the group; she, George, Christine, Diane, Kathy, and Jeanne served on steering committees. And Mary did that too plus outreach, meeting facilitation, and she still produces our newsletters. Thank you to everyone involved.

We started with a planning meeting, including the steering committee and some local bereaved parents. Sitting in a circle, we each introduced ourselves and shared a short version of our situation and how we lost our children. Then we discussed what sort of support for bereaved families was available locally and what our options might be to enhance that. We discussed the possibilities of running our own independent support group vs. starting a chapter of a national group called The Compassionate Friends (TCF).

Shortly after that planning session, I arranged for us to meet the TCF regional coordinator for our area, and that meeting went well. We decided to start a new TCF of Greater Newburyport, Massachusetts chapter because TCF provided more and varied resources than we'd likely be able to provide on our own. There were no existing chapters within an hour drive then. We found a lovely place for non-denominational meetings in the parish center of the church which hosted Brent's funeral. We held our first chapter meeting within one week of the first anniversary of Brent's death. It was significant and emotional for all of us; we felt it meaningful that we were with others who could truly understand. Now almost ten years and hundreds of bereaved families later, the chapter still meets monthly, has annual candle lightings plus occasional special events and three physical memorials to all of our deceased children, plus bimonthly newsletters.

Reaching out to others has helped me to heal and to better understand other bereaved families' struggles. It is an important part of my journey.

Not long after turning fifty, I began to search for more meaning in life, to understand what had happened, and how everything fit together, if it did.

Was there really an afterlife? I took up spiritual reading and learned meditation. I relied heavily on family and friends who listened while I talked about Brent's death and my feelings about it or told me of their feelings about afterlife and spirituality.

Bob and I took very different journeys as we coped with our grief. Bob became more withdrawn, skeptical and angry—difficult for both of us. He is creative and found some solace in writing poetry and his theater activities. His poetry was very good, quite moving, and I loved reading it—as sad as it was. It really portrayed how sorrowful he felt.

A few months later, Bob started his own acting studio and "black box" theater, a longtime passion of his. I believe that he felt it was important to do something that he cared about. After what we had gone through, it was now obvious to both of us what the phrase "life is too short" meant.

Though Bob participated in some of our early meditations, he was uncomfortable with my increasing focus on spirituality and began to pull away from me. We had difficulty understanding and appreciating each other's approach to grief and were clearly in different places in our mourning. I was still bargaining with God, not for Brent's life any longer, but for the survival of my family. Bob and I were now on even rockier ground in our marriage.

Brad reacted differently than either of us. As a sibling, he had his own unique personality and relationship to Brent. He became more withdrawn and seemed resigned to the loss. He didn't want to talk about his feelings as much as we did. But I'm sure he was lonely too.

We each expressed our anger differently and at different periods. I was an optimist while Bob was pessimistic by nature, and perhaps that may have had something to do with our different reactions. For a while, I was angry at God but not at other people. However, my anger didn't last long. Bob went through a much more pronounced and protracted period of anger than I did. He also kept many of his thoughts and feelings to himself; he didn't get them out in the open and discuss them like I did. He was very private, but I think that made it harder for him. His anger had an impact on his health, his business, and our marriage. I think Bob questioned strongly why this had to happen to him, his family, his son. I don't remember feeling singled out in that way, but I hear it is a common experience for bereaved parents.

Brad seemed to have a lot of anger at first, but like mine, his faded although not as quickly. Brad's grief manifested itself in his flunking out of college his freshman year. He had begun to behave differently than he ever had before; there were a couple of troubling incidents related to skipping classes, lying, and money; his grades were suffering.

I worried that Brad might be involved in drugs and that he didn't care about his future. After he flunked out, I pushed him into seeing a counselor, but he only went twice, probably just to quiet me. Bob and I were forced to have some very difficult tough-love conversations with him. Over time, Brad seemed to listen and get control. He was accepted back into college on probation the next fall. I was grateful . . . and relieved.

Brad later told me that he also felt the strongest grief when everyone left after the funeral then again starting school. His friends had helped distract him over the summer, but their support declined when he went off to culinary college. Once there, he wasn't interested in facing new challenges and meeting people, especially where he was naturally shy. Brad was not motivated to strive for good grades, to wear neat, ironed chef's uniforms, or even attend classes. His withdrawal grew worse until it came to a head when he had to leave college for lower than minimum grades; he could not hide his problem any longer.

With Brad away at college, Bob and I became empty nesters for the first time. The boys' absence made both the house and our lives together seem empty. We were still struggling daily with profound grief. Bob was also struggling to figure out what he wanted the rest of his life to look like, personally and professionally. I believe that just as he wasn't able to tolerate his job any longer, he couldn't tolerate being unhappy in our marriage. I realized that only much later. At the time, it felt like I was enduring another death—the death of my long-term marriage.

During the nine months after the funeral, Bob became increasingly distant. I sensed that he might be seeing someone else, and the suspicion hurt; but he denied it, saying it was just a kindred friendship with an adult student whose sister was dying of cancer. So I distracted myself with my new job and its required travel, which served as a good escape.

Finally, I pushed Bob to tell me the truth about what was going on. He only admitted that he was thinking of leaving. We'd separated twice before in our thirty years of marriage, but we had done a lot of work to restore and strengthen our relationship. I'd thought we had reached more solid ground. We were not without our issues, but I believed we were basically okay and had a future together; I still loved him.

When it finally sank in that my marriage was in real danger so soon after Brent's death, it was extremely devastating to me. I didn't know what to do about it or if there was anything I could do about it.

Bob and I talked a lot, trying to understand what was happening to us. I suggested counseling, but he was not interested in that. Ultimately, I realized that I had no control over him or the situation. Our lives had changed dramatically. We were both struggling to survive, to return to functional lives, and to find some glimmer of happiness again. When I realized that happiness for Bob might not include me, it was a terrible shock. My fight to save our marriage wasn't working.

I finally gave up. I traveled for work more than I had before, trying to give Bob space to decide what he wanted. But I did ask him to make a decision about our marriage by the first anniversary of Brent's death, which would occur in about three months. I could not stand the state of limbo I found myself in. The limbo was the worst part for me. If this was inevitable, I needed to get on with it, figure out what my new life looked like.

It was during this period that I bottomed out. Things finally came to a head one afternoon, just after I'd started my work with bereaved families. A local congregational church pastor invited me to a meeting regarding memorializing a sixteen-year-old girl who'd been run down by a drunk driver while walking home with her boyfriend. But the meeting was cancelled, and I hadn't gotten the notice. I was very disappointed when I arrived, waited, and no one showed.

I was in an emotional state, I needed something to focus on.

I drove home.

As I pulled into my garage, the realization hit me that my thirty-year marriage was over, two of my three sons were gone, my only remaining son was struggling, and when he returned to college, I would be living alone for the first time in my life. I would be starting over at age fifty-one. Suddenly, everything, including the future, seemed hopeless. I closed the garage door and left the engine running, thinking how easy it would be to end my misery.

That was the only time I've ever considered suicide, and thank God it didn't last long. I thought about what killing myself might do to Brad, and that he needed me. I also realized that I needed help, so I called my sister from my cell phone in my car and asked if she could meet me for a drink. I am still grateful that she answered the phone. As I backed the car out into the driveway, I realized that I'd just had a narrow escape. I reminded myself that I had a supportive family and a wonderful son to live for.

I've since heard that many bereaved parents have at least one moment like this where they are in so much pain, they consider taking their own lives. Ordinarily, I'm not one who shies away from a challenge, change, or new situations; but I'd never encountered such a total shift in my life, job, and family all at once. It was scary and overwhelming.

That was a very long day for me. I met my sister, and we talked for hours in the upstairs corner of a local bar and restaurant. We had several drinks, and I cried a lot. When we were ready to leave, her husband called and offered to pick us up and drop me off at home. I should have taken him up on that offer. But I was in such an emotional and grief-stricken state, I didn't realize how much the drinks had affected me, so I declined. I dropped Pat off and headed home, only three miles away. I hadn't even driven a half mile before I was pulled over by a police officer. He realized that I'd had too much to drink, took my keys, pulled my car to the side of the road, and ordered me into the back of his police cruiser.

He climbed in front. A metal grate separated us. That's when I totally lost it. I sat there in the backseat, sobbing uncontrollably. I was ashamed that I might have endangered someone else by driving under the influence. The alcohol I'd consumed had released all of my grief, and in a torrent of tears, I told the officer that I'd lost my son, I was losing my marriage, my life and family were falling apart—that I didn't know how I was going to get through it.

I now believe that some sort of spiritual grace helped turn the tide for me that afternoon. The policeman who stopped me happened to be the son of a woman who lived downstairs from my sister. He'd heard about my son's death, and because he hadn't yet written me up for a DUI, after hearing my story, he took pity on me. He drove me in the police car back to my sister's home, handed my keys to my brother-in-law, and told him not to let me drive again that night. Paul agreed. I slept at their house.

I feel gratitude that the officer had let me off easily and maybe I didn't deserve it, but if I'd had to cope with the punishment and embarrassment of a DUI while dealing with everything else, it may have sent me over the edge, and I might not be here now. That policeman was my angel even though he may not have known it at the time. I am so very thankful that he stopped me before I'd driven very far or done any damage. That was my low point, yes, but it was also my turning point.

The following month was very difficult. Even today May remains difficult, because Brent's birthday falls in it as well as Mother's Day (I'd spent my first Mother's Day in the hospital after giving birth to Brent), and it is the anniversary of his accident. The first year of any birthday, anniversary, or holiday is brutal for bereaved parents and family. In addition, I was also starting to grieve the impending loss of my marriage.

Around the first anniversary of Brent's death, Laura graduated from college. I went to Arizona, but it was bittersweet. It was wonderful to see her receive her degree as a landscape architect, and I was genuinely happy for her and proud of her. But seeing the ASU campus again made me recall how much Brent loved it and the time he spent there. I couldn't help think that he should have been able to graduate the following year.

At the same time, it was great to see Laura, her parents, and Brent's dog, Brutus, who lived with them at their beautiful home in Phoenix. Two of my girlfriends and I decided to do a short trip to Sedona, Arizona—a lovely healing and spiritual place—before the graduation. Maureen and I flew out on Mother's Day, and Maureen had us upgraded to first class—so thoughtful. Kathleen—who formally studied spirituality—knew the area, booked us in a log cabin in Oak Creek Canyon, and led our exploration and meditations. Bob and Brad chose to fly out a few days later just for the graduation. Together, we visited the accident site, left flowers, and a lit candle; it was very difficult and sad for us all over again. Bob returned home right away; Brad and I stayed for Laura's graduation party and flew home together the next day. I'm still close to Laura and her parents, visiting them and Brutus whenever I can.

Once home again, I asked Bob for his decision about our marriage. He told me he wanted a divorce. I wasn't surprised, but still, I was crushed. I had been holding on to a small hope that we could work it out somehow; we had done it before. I asked Bob, "Are you sure this is what you want? Aren't there any changes we could make, things we could work on to save our marriage after all this time?" He told me he was not in love with me anymore, that he was not happy and needed a change. He said he'd already tried when we separated and went to counseling several years earlier, but he was still not happy. He was sorry, he knew it was hurting me, but he needed to change his life.

Crying, I asked him where he was going to live, and he said he hadn't figured out the details, but he'd move out of our bedroom and use Brent's room starting that day. (We'd moved Brent's belongings but left the bed and wall hangings intact.) Brent's death and our separate responses to it were not the cause of our marriage breaking up, but it was certainly a catalyst. My understanding is that this is a common occurrence after the loss of a child; the marriage either gets stronger or it collapses.

After a lengthy and emotional discussion, Bob finally convinced me he'd made up his mind. He claimed it was not because of the other woman. I wanted to believe him, but I had my doubts. In any case, I finally realized there was no hope to save my marriage. I hated it, but I got used to it and let it go; I had no choice.

After our talk, he moved his things into Brent's bedroom. I asked him to be the one to tell Brad since the breakup was his decision, but I wanted to be there when he did.

When Brad came home that evening, we asked him to sit down; we wanted to talk. Brad, who had recently turned twenty, could probably tell that things had not been the same between Bob and me since Brent's death even though we tried to hide it. Still, I don't think he saw this coming, the news that his father was leaving.

As I remember it, Bob, facing his son across the kitchen counter, looked into his' eyes and said, "Brad, you've probably noticed things haven't been the same between your mother and me. It's been so hard for all of us since we lost Brent. I'm just not happy anymore, so your mother and I are separating. I'm going to move out when I find a place. Please know that this has nothing to do with you. We both love you, and I will still be in your life. You'll stay here with Mom. I'm sorry, this is my decision."

Brad's eyes filled with tears as he tried to hold them back. I sat next to him and put my arm around his shoulders. "We'll be okay," I said. "This is hard, but we'll get through it together. You will live here with me. I'm not going anywhere, and you will still see Dad often."

It was difficult to watch how much this hurt my son. He just looked down at the counter, shook his head, and mumbled, "Why? Can't you guys work it out?" Bob said, "We tried, but it just isn't working anymore."

Brad was just getting through a tough time at college, and now his family was falling apart too. He turned and hugged me then got up and hugged his father and headed upstairs to his room. On the way up, he said softly, "I need to be alone for a while."

He went out of our sight, and we heard his door close. I felt so sorry for him, but I couldn't think of anything to do or say to make him feel better. I felt terrible. Now that this was all out in the open, it seemed even more real and irreversible. Among my feelings of sadness, I felt some anger at the lousy timing.

I too went up to my bedroom and closed the door. I heard Bob leave and the front door close; the house went silent. Feeling very alone, I cried myself to sleep.

That week was Brent's first anniversary. Bob and I were trying to stay civil with each other for Brad's sake, and we three met at the gravesite on that date. Bob brought flowers and a baseball with a message for the grave, Brad and I got helium balloons on which we wrote notes with markers. Then together, hoping Brent would somehow receive these messages, we released them into the air, watching them rise into the sky until they were out of sight.

There is no underestimating how important ritual is for loved ones. Increasingly, I was finding that I needed to mark the important milestones in some way.

By then, much had shifted. For one thing, I no longer measured my life in terms of how old I was or how old my children were. I thought about things that occurred as "before" or "after" Brent's death, like BC or AD after a year number.

Having gotten past the first anniversary, Bob and I began to deal with the details of ending our marriage. We spent time walking on the beach or just sitting at home, talking and figuring out how we'd move on. How would we split our assets? Where would Bob live? How could we minimize the impact the divorce would have on Brad? This was all very painful stuff for me, but I felt the absolute requirement to finish it as quickly as possible so that I could begin to move on with my life again.

We agreed to split our assets evenly and that I would

buy Bob out of the house and get Brad through college, deducting half of his expected tuition from what I paid Bob. I was the one who had always wanted to live on the ocean and Brad was a homebody and water fan like I was. I didn't want him to have to move; he'd been through enough trauma for one year.

Bob asked if he could stay on in the house until he found a place, but I knew that I would need closure soon. We agreed he would move out by September, giving him three months to find a rental. It would also allow Brad time to get used to the transition.

That summer was a difficult time for me. I needed to get away and think, so I took a week off and went to visit friends and family on the coast of Maine. Just before Bob moved out and I left on a business trip to China in late August, we took Brad to dinner to acknowledge our thirtieth wedding anniversary on the twenty-sixth and have one last dinner together as a family. This was a mistake; it turned out to be a fairly silent, uncomfortable meal.

When I returned from China, Bob was gone; and within the week, Brad left to go back to college. Now for the first time ever, I was living alone. The house seemed cold and empty. That Bob left some of his belongings behind seemed like some sort of injustice. I couldn't stand having them in the house because it made it harder for me to move on emotionally. So I gathered his things, piled them in the entryway of our home, then called and asked him to come and pick them up. In the process of moving them, I dropped one of the heavier items and broke my foot—my first broken bone! That really ignited my anger; I must have said every expletive in the book then I had to get used to walking in a cast.

I asked that Bob be the one to file for divorce but offered to help him fill out paperwork, including drafting a one-page agreement on assets, which we both signed. I refinanced the house in my name, sold and split other assets, and gave Bob a check three weeks after he moved out. This put financial strain on me; but I needed to move on. We went through the entire process without a mediator or a lawyer, simply and quickly; the divorce was final by the spring.

Bob finally admitted to the affair after accidentally telling me that his girlfriend's husband had also moved out of their home. She was fifteen years younger than him, and from my viewpoint, being replaced by a younger woman seriously damaged my self-image. It made me wonder if I was attractive enough, young enough, or even had what it took to start over. Finally, after several months, I worked up the courage to begin dating.

I started by going with single friends to gatherings, performances, or parties. Then I gave it some thought and decided that meeting the right person at my age was basically a "numbers game." The more people I met, the more likely I'd meet the right one or at least one that I could be compatible with. So I decided to join two online dating sites. I was very comfortable on computers, so that part felt natural. It took some time to learn not to take things personally and to filter candidates who didn't seem appropriate. I used something I learned in the corporate world, to don my imaginary "Teflon suit" to let things "slide off" rather than take them personally. That helped a lot, and eventually, I could treat it like a game and not get hurt, plus the experiences often resulted in humorous conversations with my girlfriends over wine.

Once I let go of my own neediness and worried less about the outcome, I was invited on more dates. I discovered I could more than survive; I could thrive, even being over fifty. It was, however, quite a different experience that the last time I dated when I was a teenager. It was hard to meet like-minded people, and everyone had a history and therefore "baggage," including me; it colored our views. But after I got past that hurdle, I was a lot more self-confident than my younger self.

I had an entirely new journey to deal with now. The ending of my marriage felt like another death in my family. It reignited the pain from Brent, Robbie, and even my parents' deaths at a time when I was still raw from Brent's death. I became even more overprotective of Brad, which he resisted of course. I worried about the effect of the divorce so soon after his brother's death.

BRAD'S JOURNEY

Brad had always been an avid animal lover and wanted all sorts of pets growing up, but we'd only let him have fish and one lizard because his father was allergic to cats and dogs and disliked other animals. Finally, after years of searching, we'd found a wonderful miniature schnauzer for the boys. For sixteen years, Gizmo was a beloved part of our family. But during Bob's last summer at home, I gave Brad permission to bring home a six-week-old kitten from the litter that my niece Kim's cat, Oreo, gave birth to. Brad chose the wildest kitten, who had a vertical white stripe on its forehead, and he named it Scarface, thinking that it was a male. It turned out to be a female, but she still lives up to the name. We were fond of her, and having her around seemed to help a little. I hoped that Brad would be distracted by her when Bob moved out.

Brad worked at the small cafe across the street, preparing to reenter college. He continued working there on weekends after he went back to school. It was nice to see him often, and it helped with my initial loneliness.

That fall, when Brad returned to college, he took advantage of this second chance and focused more on school. We developed an even closer mother-son relationship; it was almost like we were peers in some ways. We took a couple of trips together, including a long weekend cruise to the Bahamas for his twenty-first birthday. The trips seemed a bit odd without Bob, but we were starting to reshape our lives. I was also starting to date, which felt very strange for me after so many years of marriage.

Watching Brad start to recover and flourish helped me along on my own healing journey; and I began to worry a little less about him.

Brad still had some tough times; he missed his Dad even though he saw him regularly. He still missed his brother, and while he was doing better, it was still difficult for him to focus on school. I sensed that he may have had some regrets about things that had happened between them. One thing that seemed to give him comfort was driving Brent's car. Shipping it back East was expensive, but it was important to us to keep Brent's car in the family. Having a car on campus made it easier for Brad to get around, return home on weekends, and made him feel closer to Brent.

One day he called me from school, very upset. Brent's car had been stolen although it had been locked and in a campus parking lot. The police found it a few days later, stripped down to the metal. Even the engine was missing. Brad was furious, and both Bob and I were sad over it. That car had been in the family a long time and had been part of Brent's life; now it too had been taken from us. We become very attached to the things that once belonged to our deceased children.

Brad went on to earn his degree in culinary arts. After graduation, when he was twenty-three, he bought the café he'd worked in throughout his college years. As an owner/chef, he was now managing employees, ordering supplies, and running a small restaurant, another difficult transition that required a tremendous amount of hard work.

The cafe gave him a new focus and a sense of accomplishment as he continued to recover from his brother's death. Like many other surviving children, Brad had lived in the shadow of a deceased sibling, but now he was moving out of that shadow. This often occurs either because that sibling may have been a high achiever or because we tend to remember the deceased's personalities and accomplishments as "iconic." It can be pretty hard for a surviving sibling to compete with an inflated memory and deal with their own grief. They might even harbor resentments regarding their parents' focus on their deceased brother or sister. I've heard of this happening in cases when there was a long illness preceding that death, which required most of the parents' attention.

Brad had a difficult time in those early years, but he overcame it and matured into a smart, handsome, loving man. I was and am very proud of him, as is his father, his stepfather, and the rest of our extended family. I am also grateful for the way his life has turned out.

THE HOLIDAYS AND ANNIVERSARIES

Every subsequent holiday and anniversary after losing a child is a new challenge, especially the first year. You don't know what to expect or how to deal with it, and you feel the grief again as if it were fresh and new. Over the years, it becomes less intense, but it's always there, sometimes a sharp reminder that can cause a setback. Ritual sometimes helps; having memorials, releasing balloons or butterflies, or just bringing flowers to the grave—whether just immediate family or a larger group. It can also help to take time out to reflect or meditate. There are no rules here; just do whatever works best for you and your family or what you think your child in spirit would like. No need for a memorial event to be elaborate or expensive, just something meaningful to you. In our support chapter newsletter, we remember the children in their birthday and "angel-versary" month; this seems to provide a little comfort. Parents are welcome to place a picture or comment on a special "Love Gift" page; they often do.

Every year you think it will get better, easier somehow; usually it does, but there were times I got nailed with a setback. As I'd mentioned, my first year was the worst, some say their second year is. I felt somewhat better after three years, but there was a temporary setback for the fifth anniversary of Brent's death. It didn't last as long as the first couple of years, but I felt lonely and depressed, was sensitive, cried easily, and missed him more than usual. The seventh anniversary was the same Friday/Sunday configuration of his birthday and Mother's Day, and that bothered me. Some years might be more difficult than others because of something else happening in the family, like a sibling wedding. I hear universally, and it is my experience, that grief lessens as time passes; even grief as intense as caused by the death of a child. It is often said that it never goes away completely, but I do think that as we learn to focus more on the love and the special moments we had with that child rather than the loss, it makes a huge difference. I've personally lost parents, grandparents, aunts, uncles, and my long-term marriage. The pain associated with those faded for me in a much shorter time than the loss of my children.

The death of a child is different, unnatural. It rocks your world in a completely different and more permanent way.

INCREASED ABILITY TO HANDLE THE UNEXPECTED

However, an interesting skill acquired from making it through the death of a child is the ability to handle other surprises or tough situations more easily than you otherwise would have. You gain a different perspective and fewer things rattle you, or they bother you less than they otherwise would have. My next big surprise came two years after Brent's death. I found that I had a half-brother seven years older than I; neither my sister nor I had any idea he existed.

Apparently, my father had a relationship with Rose in Portland, Maine, while he was in the Merchant Marines, and he fathered a son. Dad decided not to break up his original family, and it was all kept secret throughout his life. Michael was in his thirties when his mother admitted the truth to him. He mailed a letter to our father in Massachusetts but followed through on his plans to move his family to Washington state for unrelated reasons. We do not know if Dad ever received the letter. When Mike returned to Maine several years later, he came back to Plum Island with hopes of meeting his father in person. He stopped in a small local restaurant for coffee. Coincidentally, the woman behind the counter, Leah, was my best friend growing up. She'd spent a lot of time at my house and loved my father. In answer to Mike's questions, she told him that Dad had passed away but had two daughters. However, when she asked him why he wanted to know, Leah became defensive and wouldn't tell Mike the dates of my father's death, his daughters' married names, or where we lived.

Mike was very disappointed at not being able to meet his biological father but wanted to find his half sisters. He began a long search for us but did not succeed until after my mother died years later. Mike respected my mother enough not to ask her directly, not knowing if she was aware of the situation. During a subsequent visit to Plum Island, he found out she'd died and contacted my sister through Mom's neighbor.

My sister Pat and I met Mike and his wife Lynn on Thanksgiving weekend at my home, after we'd spoken briefly on the phone. Our parents were all deceased, so we had to piece things together on our own. Mike had a picture of my father holding him as a baby, and he knew many specifics about Dad's likes, dislikes, and military history. It was an interesting discussion, and we could sense he was genuine.

We felt it very likely that we were indeed related, but we all wanted to sleep on it and keep in touch. After two weeks, Mike called and asked me to participate in a DNA test with him. I agreed, and it confirmed at ninety percent that we shared a parent. Since then, we've all become quite close, with Mike, Lynn, their four children—Mike, Amanda, CJ, Matt—and their families. At least this surprise had a pleasant outcome.

Three years after Brent's death, I met Jim on Match.com. I could tell within a few weeks that he was different, and when we met in person, we hit it off immediately. He was positive, had values similar to mine, and he was a true gentleman; I liked it that he was also tall, handsome, and had three grown children, Melanie, Matthew, and Christopher that I got along with right away. He proposed after six months, and we were married six months after that. We included all my family and his in the wedding. It was a wonderful celebration of new beginnings.

Bob has remained with the same woman, and four years after Brent's death, they had a son together. Coincidentally, he was born six weeks earlier than his due date, on the day before Brent's birthday. I think at first this bothered me; I'm not sure whether it was jealousy or hurt.

Over time, however, I realized that his decisions were none of my business. In fact, the new baby turned out to be one of the best things that could have happened for Brad; he become an older brother. For years, he'd been a younger brother then tragically, an only child.

Although none of us have any control over our partner's lives after the death of a child, we are, however, probably more emotionally sensitive regarding one another after having experienced that level of grief together. I think death bonds you forever in some way, positive or negative, regardless of whether you remain together or not.

There were more trials to come. Six years after Brent's death, I was unexpectedly laid off (they said retired) from my job at IBM after ten years. I found myself in danger of losing my home; refinancing for the divorce had left me with a large mortgage payment. I loved my home on the ocean. I'd known the minute I walked through the door that it was where I wanted to spend the rest of my life. So when I didn't think I could afford to keep it, I was hurting from yet another loss. It was a very tough decision to put it on the market. Six months later when it didn't sell, I was grateful. I needed to get creative. I found a good online site for vacation rentals and created a listing to rent the house weekly during the summer.

Jim and I moved into a smaller home nearby, temporarily, using the differential in the rental income to help pay the mortgage. The economy had crashed, and jobs were scarce; but I'd decided that I wanted to derive my income from something meaningful, which could also help others. I obtained a nutrition virtual franchise from a company with integrity and high-quality products along with a mission to help others, which included providing free whole-food nutrition to children. It helped but was not enough. We continued to rent and move in and out of our home multiple times each year while I continued to look for additional ways to supplement my income. I became quite efficient at moving and tried several methods of income generation; some worked and some didn't.

A surprise that I became aware of late in the first year after Brent's death—but it took years to play out—was the possibility that Brent had left a son behind. It seemed unlikely, but I was driven to confirm or deny the existence of a possible grandchild, any continuation of Brent. One of Brent's baseball teammates, while working at a gas station and filling my gas tank, mentioned that his friend Linda told him that Brent fathered her son while in high school. He did not know if Brent knew about the boy or that Linda later died at twenty of a drug overdose. Her parents were raising the boy.

I couldn't believe what I was hearing. It seemed especially unlikely because we'd never heard Brent mention this girl, and we felt we knew most of his friends. But I couldn't let it go. I left the gas station and returned some days later to ask more questions, but he was no longer working there. I found out where he was working and went to ask for more details, but he only knew her name and the town she grew up in, not her parents or child's names or anything else. Her last name was a common one; there were too many in local phone books to call. I started to track the family down, not knowing what I'd do or how they'd react if I found them.

I asked a friend who had the same last name if she knew of any family stories similar to this; she did not. I went to the town library and looked through several years of high school yearbook pictures and finally found Linda's freshman picture, she'd overlapped at high school one year with Brent. Then I went to the town hall looking for birth certificates or obituaries, with no luck. When I couldn't make forward progress, I let it go for a while, but eventually, some thread would appear and get me restarted.

I eventually figured out that she'd been in a temporary home for teenage mothers nearby. I went to ask them about her, and they gave me a copy of the obituary they had on file for her, which told me her father's name. That led me to find his address and phone number. After thinking about it for a long time, I held my breath and called them in early December, seven and a half years after Brent's death. I talked with Linda's stepmother, Nancy, starting the conversation related to Linda's death and my role in The Compassionate Friends, but the gist of what I was looking for was revealed on the phone, and they agreed to let me come to their home, meet them, and talk. I was both thrilled and afraid, not knowing what to expect.

I found their home in Salisbury, Massachusetts, and knocked on their front door. Nancy invited me in and introduced me to Peter, Linda's father and Joshua, Linda's son. They were very nice and told me Linda's story of how she'd gotten involved with the wrong crowd and became an addict in her teens. She'd gotten clean near the end of her life but had a big disappointment: then fell off the wagon, resulting in an overdose at age twenty. It was very sad.

Earlier, at seventeen, Linda had come to them with her then boyfriend, also named Brent, aged fifteen, and told them she was pregnant. She decided to keep the child and got into the home for teenage mothers to help her stay drug-free during the pregnancy. Nancy and Peter helped her and adopted her son Joshua at six months old, then raised their grandson as a son. The other Brent that they believe is his biological father went into hiding, refusing a paternity test; his parents also refused DNA tests. That left Joshua, now eleven, feeling rejected and wanting to know more about his father. Then I showed up, telling him I've been looking for him for six years!

After hearing their story, I was disappointed. It was unlikely Josh was my Brent's son or my natural grandson even though he looked a lot like my Brad. With the caveat that it was not probable, we all agreed to have a DNA test done and prove it either way. We hoped that it proved he was my family after all, but I told him I would not disappear; I'd be his "adopted" grandmother. We had a Y chromosome test done with Brad, which should match as all males with the same father lineage would have the same one.

We talked, visited, and got to know each other's families while we waited on pins and needles for the DNA results. The results came back just before Christmas Eve— negative. Sadly, Josh was not my biological grandson. I'm not sure yet why the universe drove me to meet him and his family, but I know now there must be a reason. We stay in touch and get together to celebrate birthdays, holidays, and more. We have fun and enjoy each other's company. Joshua is a wonderful young man, in high school now and doing well. I'm delighted to have him as part of our family; it's not just bloodlines that make a family.

Another significant challenge the following year: I took a bad fall on a wet floor in the restroom of a gym facility. With my total weight and forward momentum, my feet went into the air, and I came crashing down on my head onto a solid ceramic tile floor This caused a detached retina of my dominant right eye, my "good" eye (I'd been born with a "lazy muscle" in my left eye). I didn't realize it at first, but over time, I started to notice difficulties seeing, and it took months to discover the problem.

Within a few days of discovery, I had surgery at Massachusetts Eye and Ear hospital in Boston followed by a painful ten days' facedown just before that Christmas Eve. It took a month of headaches to adapt to using only my left eye, which was functional, but less so. Two more minor surgeries followed within six months but failed to improve my sight. I learned to manage; I can drive, read, and write with the assistance of stronger lighting and magnification.

I continued doctor checkups, hoping my eye would heal. On what would've been Brent's thirtieth birthday, I learned that I was permanently blind in my right eye.

I learned something through all these challenges: life's hurdles no longer seem insurmountable. I have a more positive perspective and more confidence in my ability to handle surprises and challenges. I truly feel that I am so strong, that nothing can keep me down for long; nothing is or will be as hard as what I've already been through. It has helped me to better understand what matters. Decisions are easier, I'm less judgmental, I no longer waste time on negative things or people. I also really appreciate Brad, Jim, my step-children, my extended family and friends even more. Life is too short and too precious!

I think many bereaved parents gain this strength whether they realize it or not. We go from not knowing how the world can possibly move on without our child to an expanded sense of confidence in knowing how strong we've become even though none of us would have chosen this method to get there.

Chapter 8

My Spiritual Journey

ONCE I HAD children, I strongly believed that my primary job as a parent was protecting my children. When Brent and Robbie died and I could no longer do that for them, it was devastating, heartbreaking.

The feeling was even stronger when it came to Brent because we'd reared and protected him for twenty-one years. I'd have given anything just to confirm that he was safe and that his spirit continued on in some form.

Prior to losing Brent, I'd never spent much time thinking about life after death. I'd just accepted losses and grieved when someone I loved died. But I couldn't do only that. Not with Brent.

I didn't really know what I believed about what my friends called "spirituality." What a nebulous term. What did it mean? I'm still not sure there is a clear definition. I just know that for me, it is mostly a feeling having to do with a belief in a world beyond what we can see and understand. I remember feeling mystified and curious, yet doubting, trying to keep an open mind. But I was conflicted as a result of all the religious teachings I'd heard growing up and the skeptical views of many of my family and friends. As a parent, I needed to try to seek some answers, to find something I could believe in, some hope that Brent's spirit might still exist.

This spiritual journey started, even though I did not recognize it then, soon after his death. A couple of my friends more in tune with their connection to the spiritual world were receiving what seemed like signs from my son. Two close friends, Marc and Kathleen, separately, had odd things happen in their homes in Massachusetts at the time of Brent's death in Arizona. Marc's dog barked at the door like there was someone there precisely at the same time of Brent's death, but no one was physically there. Kathleen had some unusual issues with her office electronics right at the same time, and she could feel Brent's presence and confusion. Then Mary had a reference to Brent in automatic writing after the accident but before we took him off life support. We'd also had a few minor experiences during the week of his wake and funeral that caused us to question his continued presence, like lights flickering, candles coming back on, butterflies appearing—all at meaningful times. I'll cite significant examples later in this chapter. The point is that my mind was starting to open up to the idea of Brent possibly continuing on in sprit.

Then two months after his death, when we went to visit Bob's family in Pennsylvania, a friend of my sister-in-law's gave me a book on after-death communications, entitled *Love Beyond Life* by Joel Martin and Patricia Romanowski. The book began with scientific skepticism and contained many examples of after-death contact, which had been corroborated by multiple sources. Reading this gave me hope that Brent's spirit was living on and that he had ability to communicate with us in some way. It made me more open to the idea of looking for signs. But I was still a little skeptical.

I remember a low point around four months after his death. It happened while I was walking the beach with an empathetic friend, Leslie. We paused in our conversation and sat down in the sand. As I described to her how empty I felt, sobs racked my body, and pain came pouring out, but she didn't shy away. She shared her spiritual beliefs with me about an afterlife and how we are all connected in the universe. A short time later, she gave me a book called *Many Lives, Many Masters* by Dr. Brian Weiss, a prominent psychiatrist whose scientific background gave his ideas more credulity; he'd explored the concept of reincarnation.

I'd always had some vague beliefs in an afterlife but had never visited a psychic, medium, or spiritualist of any kind. I had not believed in reincarnation, probably because of my Catholic upbringing. I'd never really pondered either possibility seriously until losing my child.

Around the same time, three different friends told me separately about a medium named Pat, who lived near my home. Coincidentally, each friend shared a similar story. Pat had approached each of these people at different times and had given them messages from loved ones who had passed on. It turned out that my friend Leslie also knew her. Pat was retired and undergoing chemotherapy for lung cancer, but Leslie reached out to her, and Pat agreed to see me. I was both fearful and excited about this meeting.

My reading with Pat was scheduled for a Sunday. She

called me the Thursday before and introduced herself. She asked if I talked to Brent mentally and advised me to ask him to get help to learn how to "get through" to her and to be present at our scheduled session. She seemed very nice and very normal on the phone. Of course, I thought about Brent nearly constantly and spoke to him often, but I had no idea whether he was really hearing me. I certainly hoped so.

I asked him to do what Pat suggested and then also asked my parents, who'd passed away years earlier, hoping they would join our session. Bob, at first, was reluctant to participate; but he joined me at the last minute, just as I was leaving to meet Pat.

It was late October, cool and clear outside. We found her small house only a half mile from ours on the Plum Island tidal basin. We knocked, and a slight woman with short gray hair answered the door and welcomed us in. I suppose that I half expected her to look like a carnival gypsy, dressed in bold colors, in a room with a crystal ball on the table, playing strange music in an exotic atmosphere. Instead, we entered a small cozy kitchen and living room with a wood-burning stove and windows overlooking the water. Pat, dressed in a plaid flannel shirt and jeans, sat down between us at a small table.

She explained what we should expect. She would hold our hands and concentrate until she made a connection with the "other side." If she asked us any questions, she wanted short answers so that she could relay them rapidly, allowing her to also hear answers from the spirits.

The session began, and we listened intently; the ninety minutes seemed to pass quickly, given the large amount of information she revealed. I remained cautious but open, and I am convinced that Pat did get through to Brent. Bob, frowning at first, seemed skeptical. What he and I both agreed on was that Pat somehow knew too many details that she had no other way of knowing—personal things about Brent and my parents, all of whom came through in the conversation. She didn't repeat their actual dialogue but paraphrased her understanding from them, which she explained came to her in words, sounds, pictures, or feelings.

She knew the kind of music my mother liked and verbal expressions that my father always used. Even some of my aunts and uncles seemed to enter briefly. Pat also seemed aware of incidents that had happened recently at our home. She knew details about the funeral that I didn't even remember but that Bob later verified. As if to validate the entire experience for Bob, a man that he had served with in the air force appeared to Pat.

It truly felt like we were communicating with Brent and others through her. A little cryptic, but their comments seemed easy and genuine—just questions and answers with a lot of validation that made us understand who they were or what they were referring to. We were crying one minute then laughing the next—our emotions all over the place. It was quite a profound experience.

Pat said things to us that were heartening and offered some consolation. She assured us that Brent's spirit did exist, and that he was fine. Because his death had been sudden, there had been confusion in his transition, but Bob's mother had been with him at his accident scene, and my father and my childhood dog Asa had greeted him on the other side. This was good to hear although I'd never thought about animals having spirits. Pat said that Brent was trying to give us signs by moving objects in our house, but we hadn't noticed. She mentioned that finding new pennies in unusual places or changes in the intensity of lights or candles might be indications that he was present also.

Admittedly, it was a strange new experience for us, but I felt in my gut that we really had communicated with Brent, and this was a huge relief. The next day, Bob told me that he noticed I'd slept peacefully through that night for the first time since Brent's death, four months earlier.

I was so very grateful to Pat. I wanted to do more than merely pay her fee. I noticed she'd had a cord of wood delivered in a heap in her front yard. Over the course of two days, Bob and I went over and stacked the firewood neatly around both sides of her shed. It felt like the least we could do; she was noticeably weakened by her illness and unable to do the work herself. She had not been at home, but I heard later from Leslie that Pat guessed that we'd probably stacked the wood, and she was grateful. Unfortunately, cancer finally got the best of her during that winter, and we never saw her again.

She'd given us a wonderful gift. That session was the real beginning of my healing. I felt as though someone had lifted a thousand pounds from my shoulders. I understood that not everyone would believe what we had experienced. I could neither explain it clearly nor prove that it was what I believed it to be, but that didn't really matter. I believed it, and it helped. I hadn't yet realized it, but Brent's death had catapulted me into a spiritual journey that would last for years, and in fact, is still ongoing.

Meditation was one of the next steps in my journey. One of my dearest spiritual friends is Marc, a shaman and energy healer. He has been very supportive and instrumental in my spiritual journey. Six months after Brent died, Bob and I went on a getaway to St. Thomas just before the holidays with a group of theater and spiritual friends including Marc, Kathleen, Kyle, Patti, Bill, and Deb. It helped us put some distance from the "in-your-face" grief we experienced at home. We were now distracted by warm-weather activities and friends, but it was also an important part of my spiritual journey. I asked Marc to teach us to meditate on that trip.

The eight of us shared two large rooms with adjoining doors and balconies overlooking the Caribbean. Most mornings, we took part in group meditations in that beautiful spot, and we'd discuss them afterward. During those early meditations, it would take some time to center and breathe deeply, to settle into a quiet state of mind; but after some practice, I could do it. I found that centering reduced stress and allowed me to feel closer to Brent. In St. Thomas, I could feel his presence, almost like a warm hug. I suppose it's normal to doubt what you feel, and at first, I did. That is when I received one of my most memorable signs from Brent, through Kathleen's meditation.

When we went around the circle after our group meditations, Kathleen explained how clearly she saw, heard, and felt Brent. She described two significant things: the first, an image of the flowers he'd given me for Mother's Day earlier that year—but the second was what really convinced me. She said Brent seemed impatient, wanting to show her something while she was focused on her own meditative thoughts and making him wait. That was very much like him. Then he handed her the object and left. When she looked at what he'd handed her, she didn't know what it was. When she described it to me later, I almost fell off my chair. I knew exactly what it was! Kathleen had just described the ASU lanyard keychain that I'd put in his casket just before we'd closed it when no one else was around. I had not told anyone about it, not even family. Yet Kathleen, having no idea of what it was, described it in detail. That was a significant indication to me that my son's spirit still lived. What a relief!

I spent a lot of time talking to Marc on that trip, learning about his view of spirituality, including energy: chakras, the body's energy centers; auras, a luminous field of radiation surrounding a person depicting power or holiness; and so many things that were totally new to me. I'd never slowed down enough to even know of their existence, nor had I a pressing reason to care. Now I was hungry to learn, hoping to make better sense of my son's death.

During that trip, I took many notes. In a darkened room, Marc read my aura. He interpreted the colors from my chakras, telling me that he saw clear colors, especially strong in the heart chakra (love) and the crown chakra (divine). I was embarrassed when he told me I was destined to do something significant to help others. In my state of grief six months after Brent died, I couldn't even imagine what I might do that would help others. He taught me to think more openly about life and death, the significance of energy flow, the spiritual world, and how we are all connected. Marc was so very helpful in my initial healing, as were my supportive friends. After we returned home, the six of us from Massachusetts continued meeting for weekly group meditations. Although Bob participated initially, he phased out of it. He had never been as much into spirituality as me, and we were already grieving differently, starting to drift apart.

We returned from St. Thomas mid-December and endured a very painful first Christmas at home without Brent, during which we lost power and heat due to a severe snowstorm. The three of us huddled around the fireplace with a dark Christmas tree in a dark house, enduring it together. It seemed fitting somehow. The next day, Bob, Brad, and I went to Pennsylvania to visit Bob's family. We needed to see them and talk with them in more detail, just as we had with my family at home. That's how we spent most of our time there; the process was very therapeutic and cathartic for everyone to further acknowledge the reality of Brent's death and how much we all missed him.

Before we left home, I'd told Bob's sister, Donna, about my experience with the medium on Plum Island. She was intrigued. She said that her daughter Allison, who was a few years younger but had a close relationship with Brent, had experienced some signs from him as well. Donna was still grieving the death of her mother several years earlier and wanted to try a reading from a medium but didn't want to go alone. I asked if she could get a referral from friends, having been advised that you should always be referred to make sure you were seeing a genuine spiritualist.

Through someone she worked with, Donna found a medium named Lauri in the Allentown area. I called to make an appointment when we got to Pennsylvania. Even over the phone, Lauri started to pick up things about me, aspects of my work, without me disclosing anything personal. The next day, Donna, her daughter Allison, my son Brad, and I went to the reading at Lauri's house. Bob and his father declined to join us.

Lauri's home was lovely and still beautifully decorated for Christmas. She was young, probably in her thirties.

She explained that she had small children and worked from home. She seemed very "normal" and invited us to sit around her dining room table. I'd learned from my first experience that it is hard to write down what you are experiencing and harder to remember all the details later, so I'd asked her if we could bring a tape recorder, and she said that was fine. We brought two portable recorders and two tapes, so Donna and I would both have one. The odd thing was that we could not get either of them to function even after installing new batteries in both. Lauri said that that sometimes happened, that the energy in the room didn't allow it. One could be coincidence, but both?

OK, that was a little weird, but not scary, and so we got started. Brent came through again, telling Lauri things to identify him, which she could not have known, like details about his military school or particular likes and of course, his style of comments. My mother-in-law Fran (Donna and Bob's mother), who had died from skin cancer sixteen years earlier, made herself known too. Lauri told us many things about her that validated her continued existence, things that we'd not revealed, such as how she looked and the style of clothing she wore especially during her illness. Lauri also mentioned some endearments that only Donna knew. Donna was crying softly but clearly happy to hear from her mother. Brad and Allison were wide-eyed but intent and quiet.

The thing I remember most about that meeting was Lauri asking me if I knew someone named Kathleen. She said that Brent found her easy to talk to, that Kathleen had natural ability, and should consider offering readings. I was amazed! Kathleen is the very good friend I mentioned earlier who had given me several messages from Brent since his death. She's a nurse by profession—very spiritual and, apparently, has psychic capabilities. Perhaps this was inherited, as she mentioned her father and grandmother had these skills as well. She's never done anything professional with her paranormal abilities. Kathleen is very genuine and caring. I found it amazing that Lauri would single her out.

Bob wasn't very happy that I was attending these sessions and encouraging his sister to go; I think his father thought we were crazy. I didn't care. If there were an opportunity to get a message to or from my son, I was going to take it!

We spent more than an hour with Lauri. Donna seemed relieved to get confirmation from her mother. Allison and Brad, both teenagers at the time, seemed fascinated and happy that they'd come with us. My faith in the afterlife was growing, and a small rip was appearing in what had been the solid fabric of my grief. When we got home, Bob and his father listened to us without much interest. They were not believers—no surprise, no problem.

Around this time, I felt compelled to get a tattoo in Brent's honor. I'd never wanted one before, but now it felt important to do before the year ended in which my son died and in which I turned age fifty. All that I knew for sure was that it had to be a butterfly, a symbol of transition. Spontaneously, while visiting Brent's grave one day, I'd taken a rubbing of the butterfly we'd etched into his gravestone even though it was too large for a tattoo. Nevertheless, with a pencil and piece of paper from my backpack, I held the lined white paper to the vertical stone and quickly scraped the pencil back and forth over the stone so that the indentation of the etching came out as a white butterfly amidst the dark gray pencil shading. I folded it and put it in my purse, not knowing what I would do with it.

I've never been a fan of tattoos, but while we were in Pennsylvania, I told my sister-in-law that I wanted to get one in memory of Brent. My niece said she wanted one too, and so did Brad. He'd gotten his first tattoo in Las Vegas on that last weekend with his brother. After that, a friend of his designed one in honor of his brother with a flaming cross, the initials BRD that both Brent and Brad shared (Brent Robert DeLibero and Brad Ryan DeLibero), and the years of Brent's birth and death. It was lovely but done in black. He wanted to upgrade his tattoos with color.

So on December 29, my son, my niece, her boyfriend, and my sister-in-law went out looking for a tattoo parlor in an area of town that my niece knew they existed. I wanted to find a clean place with a talented artist who could complete mine before the year ended. We found several places. The owners and tattoo artists were quite the cast of characters: some bald with tattooed faces or necks, some with long stringy hair or beards and colorful tattoos covering their arms, some with lots of piercings. But they were pleasant guys and seemed to be quite talented artists.

We laughed at ourselves: the teenaged and middle-aged contingent on a search in some of the stranger parts of town. Once again, Bob and his father thought we were crazy, and said so. Everywhere we stopped, I looked through design and photo books for a butterfly that looked right, but nothing did. I finally remembered the gravestone rubbing and showed it to an artist in one of the parlors. He took it from me, traced the butterfly with a black marker to create a realistic creature, and reduced it on a copier so that it would work as a shoulder tattoo. I realized that was what I'd been searching for: a butterfly that linked me to Brent. However, he was too busy to fit me in before the end of the year, as were most of the artists.

We kept looking and tried a place recommended by one of Allison's friends. It didn't look too weird, seemed clean, and they could schedule me in time using the reduced gravestone drawing from the other artist. We negotiated a better deal by asking for combined pricing to do my tattoo and Brad's. The next day, December 30, Brad and I returned to get his tattoo done. I went with him and took pictures of the process. The first one, his tribal band, looked great in his favorite color—a beautiful shade of reddish orange outlined in black. The flaming cross designed by his friend Patrick came alive outlined in black with the flames in vibrant reds, oranges, blues, and yellows plus the initials in dark bold Old English print.

The next day, the last day of the year, Brad and I returned for my tattoo. I was a little nervous, but I needed to choose colors. I decided on the four favorite colors of family members: green for Brent, orange for Brad, blue for Bob, and purple for me. The artist blended the blue, green, and purple hues on the butterfly and outlined the black edge in orange. This time, Brad took pictures of them creating my tattoo. It hurt a little, but not much, and the butterfly came out great, lovely, and symbolic. Brad and I shared another mother-son bond while creating this memorial to Brent, which felt quite spiritual.

Back at home, the weekly meditations with our small group and occasionally a few additional friends at home were helpful. We talked afterward about our experiences, and that helped too. Frequently in my meditations, I felt Brent's presence and saw his face as well as the faces of other relatives including parents and grandparents. But even more interesting was the mix of vibrant colors and many other faces I saw but did not recognize: some human, some animal. I saw eyes—pairs of eyes—focused on me. Were they trying to tell me something? Or ask me something? Often, I could not see the entire face, just the eyes; they looked to me like the eyes of owls, tigers, snakes, or sometimes people or creatures I couldn't identify. Sometimes I doubted what I was seeing, but I wasn't trying to conjure up any of this, and I wasn't thinking of those things when it happened.

Marc led most of the guided meditations, and sometimes my visions would relate to what he was seeing, hearing, or feeling. Occasionally, his meditations related to what others in the room felt even though during the process, we were silent. Sometimes it was simply soothing, dark, and quiet.

Marc would always start with a blessing:

> *The light of God surrounds us,*
> *The love of God enfolds us,*
> *The power of God protects us,*
> *The presence of God watches over us,*
> *And wherever we are, God is.*

Then he would light a candle and burn a bundle of sage for cleansing and preparing the environment. After a while, the scent of sage instantly made me relax, which was—and still is—very handy. It also makes me want to meditate, which I know is good for me; I should do it more often. Ideally, everyone should; but for bereaved parents, I'd recommend it as a stress reducer and a healing way to feel quiet and closer to your child. Deep breathing is a secondary stress reducer if meditation is difficult at first. One 'how-to' resource is the book "Meditation for Dummies" by Steven Bodian.

The March after Brent's death, I decided to try another spiritual tool: energy healing. I knew that Marc did this, and I trusted him; but nevertheless, I didn't know what to expect. I was still hurting emotionally, and this was during a time that I was afraid my marriage was falling apart.

I tend to prefer holistic rather than medical or chemical approaches, so I set up a time to see Marc for an energy healing session.

I went to his healing room, which was very warm and scented with burning sage. He asked me to take off my shoes and lie on a soft mattress on the rug. I did that, and then he covered me with a blanket. After that, he placed several shapes, sizes, and colors of crystals on my entire torso and upper body where the chakras reside. Then he went into a kind of trance. During this trance, he began moving energy through the meridians in my body looking for blockages. These are the same meridians used in acupuncture along which Chi or energy flow.

Marc asked questions about my youth, background, and recent events, following a directed path to focus on pain points that he felt were causing some of my blocks. He seemed to be guided in the questions he asked by some unseen source. Then he worked to release the blockages he discovered in my lower legs. This was an intense and sometimes painful process since he used acupressure, but I felt the blocks release and felt amazing afterward—relaxed and peaceful. He told me to get lots of rest and drink plenty of water over the next twenty-four hours and to write down some of the things we spoke about. This should include the grief that came up that would help me process this experience. That evening, I felt better than I'd felt since Brent died. It seemed that the toxins I'd absorbed and the pain I'd endured, as well as the fear, had diminished—at least for a while.

I was very grateful to Marc and have gone to him for an energy healing session at least once or twice a year since then. I go especially when I'm experiencing a big transition. He always seems to know what I need and helps me feel better. Often, he gives me some sort of spiritual message, reminding me of something I should pay attention to or a conceptual message from his spirit guides or mine.

Not long after that, as the first anniversary of Brent's death approached, I felt the need to see another medium. I asked my friend Kathleen for a referral, and she recommended Kevin, a full-time medium who worked out of his house in Salem, Massachusetts, and occasionally out of friends' offices in Reading or Melrose, Massachusetts. Kevin, a former flight attendant and train conductor, said he had been pulled reluctantly into spiritual medium work by visitations from spirits. He's the medium I've spent the most time with, and we developed a friendship. He's very blunt, down-to-earth, and funny but also very accurate. He does not fit the stereotype;I'd never have guessed he was a medium.

I met Kevin just under a year after Brent died. I'd scheduled a forty-minute session with him and brought along a tape recorder as well as a notebook and pen—anything to help me remember what transpired in the reading. I later realized that I was still in what I call the "validation" stage, needing to be convinced that these mediums were actually talking to my son.

During my first reading, Kevin told me more in forty minutes than the others had in twice that time. He knew so much about Brent and his accident; it was uncanny. This is not information he could've gotten anywhere, certainly not from me. Most of the details hadn't appeared in the local paper even if he had had time to research it, which is unlikely since I've never even told him my last name. Kevin knew things like what make and color car Brent was driving, that he had worn a military uniform, details about his girlfriend, and all kinds of other things that really blew me away! From that first session, I was hooked.

Again, I felt relieved and even more certain that I was on the right track and that Brent and Robbie were okay. At this point, I was already in the process of starting a support group for bereaved parents, and I referred some of those parents to Kevin, hoping they would also find some relief. I even went to him with friends and took a cousin, who had lost his wife at an early age, to see him.

I probably went to him every four to six months and invited him to speak to bereaved parents that were interested in my home one at a time. Six parents decided to get readings; he helped most if not all of them.

After a while, I moved into a different phase. I needed more than just validation from a medium; I needed my communication with Brent to be more conversational, to really know more about him and how he was doing. I needed to feel that we were still connected long-term. And I wanted to develop my own skills to communicate with my son. About that time, Kevin started classes for just that: helping people develop their own "psychic" capabilities. He believed that everyone has the ability to sense psychic information on this plane. He also felt that many of us have some ability to sense or communicate with another plane, or the "other side," where the spirits have passed on. Once he'd gotten help learning to develop this skill, now he wanted to help us too.

I went to approximately three of his sessions, each six-weeks. There were typically fifteen to eighteen people in each class. We sat in a circle with a lit candle in the center, and we placed pictures of a deceased loved one in a bowl that he provided. At the beginning or end of each class, Kevin would choose three of these photographs and do a mini reading for those students. The rest of the class consisted of discussions on how to make ourselves more sensitive to psychic signals. After that, we'd have quiet time to try to see if we picked up any signals from any of the other students, and then we would discuss the experience and what we sensed.

I was amazed at how far some people progressed during that time. And I was surprised that I picked up thoughts from others in the room, but my progress was minor in comparison to theirs. I became more in touch with my intuition as part of these sessions, and I have learned to listen to and trust what I was feeling, but I was getting frustrated with my lack of ability to communicate with Brent or Robbie at will. I once asked Kevin why he thought that was, and he told me it was probably because I was too "busy" all the time. He said I didn't have enough down time, quiet time, or time to just "be"; reflect and listen. He was right. I'd gotten that same message through readings, meditation, and other events. But I still have a difficult time making myself take more quiet time even though I know it would benefit me.

Through these classes, I moved into my second phase of working with mediums, what I think of as the "conversational" phase. While I was attending sessions with Kevin, even when it was not my week for a reading, Brent would find a way to get through. This was very exciting for me. In the middle of an unrelated conversation, Kevin would say, "Your son's here again! He wants to say Hi." Then Kevin would ask something specific; for instance: "Does Singapore mean anything to you this week?"

"Yes," I said. "I was planning a trip to Singapore earlier today."

"Brent wants you to know he was there with you."

These incidents were comforting. Over time, I relaxed with certainty that Brent was fine and still checking in on me.

One particular example is especially worth noting. Kevin was interrupted by Brent who said that he had a young teenage boy with him who had hung himself.

"Do you know anyone like that?" Kevin asked. (He knew I'd started a nonprofit chapter for the support of bereaved parents.)

I thought about it. "No," I said. "I don't know anyone whose child died like that at that age. How sad."

We talked about it a little more. Kevin said that Brent was helping this young man "cross over," and he wanted the boy's parents to know that he was okay. A day or two later, I saw the story in the local paper: a fourteen-year-old boy had hung himself. As a result, I reached out and phoned his mother, Diane, now a dear friend. At the time, after expressing my sympathies and listening to her story, I hesitated to bring up the subject of an afterlife. But I thought that if this were me, I'd want to know there was hope that my son's spirit continued, and that he might be okay. So I took a deep breath and told her about Brent and my discussion with Kevin. I now know that she thought I was crazy then, because we've since talked about it many times, but she didn't hang up on me, and I was able to plant the seed of hope.

Five years after Brent's death, I met Shelia, another medium, during a psychic fair at Brad's cafe. There were several people who played games and did readings at the restaurant related to psychic phenomenon, but Shelia was clearly the most talented. In brief readings, and despite many distractions, she was accurate and succinct when she spoke about Brent and others. She was also an animal intuitive and had some comments from Gizmo, who'd recently passed away. Shelia was probably in her forties with shoulder-length light brown hair and blue eyes, with a laid-back personality, a wonderful Southern accent, and a hilarious sense of humor. That made the readings with her fun rather than maudlin.

I wanted to be able to talk with her more fully, so I scheduled a private reading with her. Her home was lovely. She took me out to a solarium with many windows, natural light, and lots of plants—a great environment and not spooky at all. She connected easily with Brent and conversed with him. She knew a lot about his personality, his likes and dislikes. She gave me messages from him and even from a few others. Brent said he was trying to help Brad through a tough time with his girlfriend and his financial situation. I'm not sure exactly how, but he wanted to make it clear he was trying to look after his brother. Most importantly, perhaps, we were able to laugh together about—and with—Brent and celebrate some of his life and attitudes, which hadn't changed from what I was hearing. She gave me hope that I could continue to converse with him by explaining that he was still himself, that his sprit would continue existing, and that he would always be available to me.

Just as I'd referred people to Kevin, I later brought other friends and family members to see Shelia. They were impressed with Shelia's ability to connect and convey information quickly and easily. That plus her easy demeanor led me to set up a group with interested bereaved parents from my chapter. This time, eight of them came to my house for individual sessions, and they told me they were all were glad they did. She ended by doing a reading for me, as we'd done before. After everyone left, we sat at my kitchen counter; Shelia had some funny comments from my cat Scarface, who was alive and there with us, that fit her personality perfectly. But the important moments that night related to my book. I'd never mentioned it, but Shelia knew I was writing a book and asked me about the title. I told her the title I was considering, but she suggested the one I did use for this book, "A Butterfly's Journey." This seemed like a message for me from the universe, and it felt right.

Approximately a year later, feeling like I was not getting much more out of my validation and conversational work with the mediums I knew, I felt like I needed to explore further, but didn't know how. Shortly after, around six years after Brent's death, a third phase that I think of as my 'healing phase' began; it really accelerated my understanding and the healing of my grief.

I met Janet by coincidence, or perhaps divine intervention, on a Wednesday, at a ladies' night event at Brad's cafe. The event was run by Deb, a girlfriend and skin care specialist. I didn't think I could attend because Jim had car problems, which required me to pick him up at work, about thirty minutes away, and then drive him to where his car was being repaired, thirty-minutes in the other direction. But when I was on the way to pick him up, he called and said a co-worker happened to have a meeting nearby and would give him a ride. That freed me to attend the event in support of Deb and Brad.

Deb brought Janet, who had at first declined but then changed her mind.

At the café, Deb introduced us; Janet seemed nice, well dressed, and very polite. As the other women arrived, I noticed that it was a smaller number than usual; there were only eight of us. We gathered around the cafe's center table. As we introduced ourselves, I mentioned that I ran a nonprofit in addition to working for IBM and was the café owner's mother. I remember thinking that was odd as I don't usually mention the nonprofit in conversations with people I did not know. The topic of children who'd passed away seemed to make strangers uncomfortable. But someone asked me what kind of nonprofit, and I explained briefly, hoping the mood wouldn't shift to a somber one. As we went around the table, Janet mentioned that she was an artist, a certified hypnotherapist, and a medium (something she later told me that she did not normally announce either). I asked to talk to her further offline, and she agreed. Later, we said we'd both felt an immediate spiritual connection.

We had a fun event over a delicious dinner that Brad and his staff made and served, accompanied by the BYOB wine, while Deb performed skincare demonstrations on some of the participants. Once Brad and his team were finished, we suggested that they go ahead home; we would clean up after we were done and lock up—I had a key to the cafe. After the other ladies left, Janet offered to help me. We cleared the table, and there was some wine left, so we shared it and sat down to talk while Deb was packing her car.

I felt a stronger connection to Janet as we spoke. By now, I was no longer stereotyping mediums and psychics, so I didn't expect her to look or act weird. On the contrary, she was a lovely woman near my age who owned a fine arts business, worked as a life coach, and had an established clinical hypnotherapy practice.

I sat on a chair at a table facing the counter. Janet sat on a stool at the counter, slightly higher and facing me where she could also see the front of the café. We started to discuss her hypnotherapy practice and work as a medium. Then suddenly, gazing over my head toward a corner of the café, she had a quizzical look on her face. She asked me if I knew a young man who might be wearing a military uniform. She said there was someone like that standing at a distance.

"Yes, that's my son, Brent!"

I was shocked and ecstatic at the same time! She told me that Brent came close to her, excited when he realized that she could understand him.

Janet described him as being tall, handsome, and fit. He was holding something red. That had to be the red plume on his army ROTC parade hat pictured in my favorite high school graduation photograph of him. She also described a kind of cocky smirk and overconfident attitude—that really felt like Brent!

Meanwhile, Deb finished packing her car and came in to relax and eat the dinner that she'd not had time for earlier. She also sat at the counter so that the three of us made a kind of triangle. As she listened to Janet and me discussing Brent's presence in the room, Deb was speechless, not ever having heard a conversation like this one.

Janet felt that Brent's death may have been an accident from a spiritual point of view rather than a planned spiritual contract end to his human life. He'd been shocked at finding himself crossing over after the accident. He was sorry for what he'd put us and Laura through.

Janet also said that Brent needed my help to "let go" so that we could both heal. My grief was holding him back, and he needed to move on in his spiritual journey. I was both surprised and disappointed at this. What did he mean by "let go"? Did he want to pull way from me? Was I smothering him or holding him back? Didn't he love me anymore or still want to be connected to me? I'd been so proud of the progress I'd made. I'd felt that I was in much better shape than most of the parents I dealt with. Had I been wrong? I felt hurt and upset; I just wanted to connect with my son, to love him, and to heal myself.

Janet explained that he'd always be with me and he would always love me. However, the intensity of grief can hold our children back because they feel "tethered" to us especially when we are in our worst stages of grief. They feel empathy and the responsibility to linger nearby to try to help us. This can hold them back. They want to see us happy just like we'd like to see them happy; they worry about us as we do about them. I'd heard enough to know that I wanted to explore this more.

I felt more deeply touched by that discussion than anything I'd experienced thus far, but it was getting late, so I got Janet's contact information and told her I'd call her. I went home feeling a deeper connection to Brent. I wrote about it in my journal, both that I was scared about changes to come and excited that I seemed to be entering a new phase in my relationship with him. My intuition told me that Janet was genuine, that she understood Brent better than anyone I'd spoken to yet.

Through several subsequent sessions with her, including some hypnotherapy and energy healing, Janet explained my family's karmic relationship, personalities, and history. She seemed to understand what we needed from each other and helped us heal on both the physical and spiritual planes.

Janet explained that each of us has a spiritual path to follow, a path that contains goals and lessons that extend beyond our human lifetime. We are embodied in this life for the purpose of learning the lessons we need for our spiritual growth. But the point is, each of us keeps striving and progressing toward our spiritual goals through multiple lives while our spirit remains the same essence or energy. The lives we live as humans relate to lessons our spirits need to learn. So in spirit, our children continue to grow and progress on their own spiritual journey just as they would in this life, growing up, and going out on their own.

If we are overcome by grief, it is as if we are ill, requiring more of their care and attention. Similarly, think about how you feel around someone really depressed. Their dark mood probably brings you down. Our grief can do that to our children as well. Healing and feeling love is better for us and for them, and it frees them to pursue their other spiritual goals.

I asked Janet, "But if I let go and heal, would we still love each other and stay in touch?" I feared losing contact with Brent or that he might be too busy to check in on me. Janet asked me to think of it as if Brent were on the other side of the world where I couldn't physically see him, but he was still a big part of my life. He would always be with me.

Although I didn't yet understand fully, I wanted to do whatever I could to help us all heal and to let Brent progress on his spiritual journey. I was just hoping that I wouldn't have to give him up in the process. As a mother, one part of me wanted to cling to anything I could hold on to him; another part of me knew I had to let go and let him "grow up" on his own journey.

Janet also reminded me about the law of attraction, which states that we all attract things at the vibration level of energy that we think, and that grief is lower, heavy energy. It is the opposite of love and joy.

Hearing this helped me to relax and listen to what Janet had to say a little less emotionally. She continued, saying that the positive shift in my energy would also help Brad and even Bob. It would bring all of us lighter energy, and it would allow Brent to move on with his spiritual path more easily. He could not fully focus forward while worried about me. Janet said Brent's current spiritual goal was somehow an extension of his earthly goal to become a pilot and something he would use to help others.

By this time, I definitely felt that it was destiny that Janet and I had met. This kind of information she gave me about Brent was not the same as the other mediums had given me. They had told me bits of information for validation of his continued existence, or they engaged in conversation with him. Janet's insight was more karmic in nature; it was the big picture of how we connected across lifetimes and our effects on each other's energy and, most importantly, our spiritual bond.

Some of the highlights of the information gained during those sessions were that Bob, the boys, and I had shared past lives in which I had enjoyed especially strong relationships with Brent and Brad. She helped me to realize why Bob needed to pull away from me for reasons having to do with his own journey, growth, and spiritual education. She made me understand that Brad's grief was deeper than I'd realized, that he'd struggled more than I knew. In both cases, their methods of dealing with grief were different, but not against me, and they were much better now. Those discussions inspired me to talk honestly with Brad. I told him what I went through while grieving, and I asked him about his experiences and listened without judgment. This exchange made us even closer.

Janet also helped me realize that Bob's fathering a son with another woman was really a good thing for Brad. That had been difficult for me to accept, but now I understood that Brad having a younger half brother was much better than him feeling lonely. Now there would be someone new who would look up to him.

I also gained some insight about my experience in losing Robbie. Janet explained that he was on his own journey and had a reason for going through stillbirth. She said that he loved me and was grateful for me, but that this wasn't quite the level of closeness that Brent, Brad, and I had achieved over the years, and that was fine. I'd been feeling guilty that my grief was not as strong for Robbie as it was for Brent.

Unborn children, Janet continued, are not meant to live on this earth for reasons related to their spiritual journey, and their parents should not feel guilty about that. This does not mean they should not grieve the loss.

Janet was able to connect me to both Brent and Robbie through separate hypnotherapy sessions. I connected with Robbie on what would have been his twentieth birthday. I saw him as he would have looked at twenty, but I knew it was him. He resembled Brent and Brad but did not look exactly like either. It was a warm and loving vision and feeling, and I felt he was fine, grateful that I'd helped him with that part of his journey. I was surprised how hard his twentieth anniversary hit me when it hadn't been difficult for some time. I never knew when grief would show up and surprise me.

When I connected with Brent, it was different, and I remember feeling more nervous like this was more crucial. It took Janet and me two or three tries to feel like I was relaxing into hypnosis. When I finally did and felt Brent, he was in an energetic, not-human form. I did not see his face but felt warmth, love, and gratitude while seeing a gray and black semitransparent netting-style blanket surrounding me. I felt a slight hesitation when it covered my head and face, but my intuition told me I had nothing to fear, and so I relaxed into it almost immediately. It was a wonderful experience; my intuition told me it was Brent, and I felt very close to him.

You need to have an open mind and some faith to

believe in these things, but I've learned to get in touch with and trust my intuition. Even though under hypnosis, I was aware enough to remember the details. What I've come to believe does not seem far-fetched to me; after all, most religions are based on faith and believe in an afterlife. Quantum physics is a science that believes everything is made of energy and is interconnected. Neurologists and neuroscientists have recently talked about their own experiences, including Dr. Jill Bolte Taylor and Dr. Eben Alexander, who totally changed their opinions on energy and afterlife. You can see videos about their experience on www.youtube.com, which are very enlightening. I now believe that I have a better, still incomplete understanding of the ongoing flow of life and spirit, and that we are each on our own journey yet connected between physical and spiritual planes.

Throughout the sessions with Janet, she and I talked more about Brent's journey. She received confirmation from him that our work was helping him, and she felt my family's overall energy shift in a positive way.

Later, I invited Janet to one of our chapter support meetings, and we received a higher-than-usual turnout. She did not charge us anything; she just wanted to help. During that meeting, she was able to tell each parent what their child was involved in on the other side. In all cases, it was related to things they loved here, yet she'd known nothing about any of them. She also attended one of our annual memorial candle-lighting ceremonies and talked with interested parents; this was helpful to them.

Sometimes parents feel guilty if they aren't always deeply sad as if their grief was an obligation, but it shouldn't be that way. Our children want to see us happy whether they are with us or not. That makes sense to me as hard as it sometimes is to lighten up and concentrate only on the love instead.

As I visited different types of paranormal practitioners, I wondered about the differences. I used to think they must be the same, all of them having all types of skills, but I came to realize that they are very different in the same way we are all different with our own unique talents. My understanding now is that the difference between psychics and mediums is that psychics focus on this plane or reality in the present and future while mediums focus on communicating with the "other side" where our beloved lost children reside although some practitioners are able to do both.

I've also learned there are three primary ways in which they receive information: (1) the clairaudient practitioners can hear the communications, (2) the clairvoyant see the communications in a kind of vision, and (3) the clairsentient intuit what is being communicated.

As I mentioned earlier, there is much faith involved in working with psychics and mediums, and they all seem to have different approaches, some better suited than others for what any given recipient needs.

I went to a few other practitioners besides those I've mentioned, but these were mostly one-time sessions and not as notable. I had good experiences except for one that I went to without a referral in a small town in Florida. That was a waste of time and money; my recommendation is to get a referral.

My spiritual journey consisted of more than mediums—a lot more. I've read books on spirituality related topics including those that would help me focus in the present rather than the past, search for my spiritual destiny, and learn to develop and trust my intuition. I also used meditation to calm me, clear my mind and help me look for signs and opportunities. I became more open-minded, learned more about the paranormal, quantum physics and other topics. I've also done many spiritual and ritualistic activities, such as tarot, full-moon fire ceremonies, writing to my angels or automatic writing, spiritual-development weekends, Shamanic Massage, Yoga, Reiki, Polarity, Reflexology and Sound Healing sessions. I also joined groups for meditation and discussions. This work has changed my life.

It's difficult to describe, but it's clear to me that over the last several years since Brent's death, I've been on a quest not only to contact Brent and Robbie and confirm their continued existence but also to learn about spirituality and what that means to me. I think that it's personal, that it means something a little different to everyone. For me, it included thinking about myself in a way that I never had before. I started to get in touch with my deepest inner feelings, to really think about what was important to me.

I also tried to take better physical care of myself and became interested and educated in nutrition. Exercise, deep breathing, eating better, including more fruits and vegetables, helped me improve my health and reduce my stress. I felt compelled to be kinder to myself, to the earth, and to others around me—including animals. I realized that you need to be good to yourself first to be able to help others. Through my nutrition franchise and their children's foundation, which gave free juiced-and-dried produce to children, my thoughts were to get to enough people to prevent a child's death. I could not track it, but even one would be worth it.

I have come to realize that this journey of loss and spiritual growth has made me a better person. I am less judgmental, more aware of myself, of others, and even of nature. More importantly, it's made me more at peace with myself and my losses.

It has also made me understand what is important in my life and what is not. I've found that the things I used to consider so important are not, like work, material things, details of my outward appearance, and doing things just because others thought I should. What is important to me now: family, friends, and helping others as well as doing the best I can at whatever I choose to do plus working at something I am passionate about.

I believe in the flow of energy or Chi through everything and that our lives are affected by how well our energy flows and how positive we are. Above all, I believe that even after the most devastating losses in our lives, with hard work, faith, and the support of friends and family, we can find peace of mind, happiness, and the forever love of our children.

Chapter 9

The Best of What I Learned

HOW DO I summarize the essence of my experience? Let me try. After enduring the loss of three children and my long-term marriage and after ten years of exploring, searching, and learning, I've come to believe that the three most important things to know while recovering from the loss of a child are:

1. be good to yourself; be open; trust your intuition.
2. helping others helps you heal.
3. it's all about the love

1a. BE GOOD TO YOURSELF

It's so easy to try to be selfless after this kind of loss and worry about everyone else, but it's very important to focus on being kind to yourself first. We cannot truly love others until we love ourselves, and we are a much better resource for others if we take care of ourselves. How to do this is not the same for everyone and will likely not be the same for your spouse or your other children.

Don't expect others to grieve like you do, to take care of themselves in the same way, or even do what you suggest. When you think others need to change, remember that you can only change yourself. Accept the fact that everyone has his or her own method of grieving, and just ask them if they need anything then let them be; give them space—and take space and quiet time for yourself.

Heavy grieving requires much introspection. We need to get in touch with how we are honestly feeling deep down. If we have anger or regrets, we need to contemplate ways to work through those feelings. At some point, we need to think through the memories of the past and what the future looks like for us and our families. We may need to work on forgiveness—of ourselves or of others; that is very important, and in either case, it frees us. We've been bruised physically and emotionally and deserve to be taken care of for a while even if we have to do it ourselves. Actually, we are the only ones who can be sure we are getting what we need. Similar to needing rest and good nutrition when we have a bad cold, we need that even more while we're grieving. We also need healing therapies and tools to help us heal our emotions. The death of a child changes your perspective on everything. Acknowledge that and give yourself plenty of quiet time and help to process it.

I found that the tools that helped me the most were meditation or deep breathing, journaling, exercise, nutrition, therapy, talking with others, holistic healing, helping others, and spiritual exploration. I'd never meditated or journaled; nor did I know much about nutrition, healing, or spirituality. I knew I needed to do something to ease the most debilitating and oppressive grief and pain I'd ever felt.

Trying to work harder at my job to keep my mind off it did not help much; rather than healing, it was just a distraction. My husband, son, and I all grieved very differently.

I followed my gut and reached out to try new things, such as meditation. Meditation took a few tries to get into but eventually became a real gift, an incredible source of peace, relaxation, and the state in which I could most often feel my sons' presence. Along with reducing my stress, it also became clear that I would receive the best ideas or solutions to questions or problems during quiet time and meditation. Ideally, it is practiced daily. I learned how from Marc, my shaman friend, then from taking more formal meditation classes from my friend Dr. Susan, and from participation and discussion with others. But I also bought the book *Meditation for Dummies* for reference on methods and results. I figured out that practice was the key. If the idea of meditation is too heavy or strange for you, as it is for some, simply practice deep breathing, which has a similar calming effect and can help you get to sleep when needed.

Sit or lie down comfortably and breathe in slowly through your nose into your diaphragm/abdomen (not your chest) to a count of four; then breathe out even more slowly through your mouth to a count of six. Repeat this twenty-five times or so; it works, can be done anywhere anytime, and costs nothing. Even just a few deep breaths can help calm a stressful time.

As I mentioned earlier, I was surprised at how cathartic I found journaling. I could write my innermost feelings and thus release them. I did not have to hold them inside or share them with anyone unless I wanted to. Journaling brought out feelings I wasn't consciously aware of and allowed me to vent, without needing any "victims" for my wrath or sadness. It felt liberating, and my journals became the basis for this book. I could go back to check on how I was feeling at certain times or to help me remember more clearly.

Exercise is good, promotes health, and eases stress. Walking was best for my moods, especially walking along the beach. It cleared my head but allowed me to think, and the energy of the water helped to heal and cleanse. Just sitting on the sand in the middle of a walk, watching and listening to the waves and seeing the sky changing, was so very peaceful and healing. Being tired from a long walk also helped me sleep.

At first, I didn't care about what I ate, nor did I have any interest in cooking. While grieving, that is normal. But after some time passed, I got interested in nutrition and learned how important it is to promote health and reduce stress. I tried to improve my diet. I started eating a lot more fruits and vegetables, cooking healthier foods, and taking whole food supplements. I learned that dark green vegetables contain tryptophan, which converts to serotonin in our brains. Low levels of serotonin may lead to depression or eating and sleeping disorders. I also came to understand that sugar, gluten (in wheat, rye, barley), dairy products, and processed food is not good for us. I always feel better when I eat well, and any progress here helps, even if it isn't perfect. I also eliminated hard liquor. I found that it was darkening my moods, and of course, liquor is a depressant. Bereaved parents certainly don't need more depression.

Therapy was well worth it. Find a therapist that you trust and respect and go to him or her for as long as you feel the need. Between Brent's death and my marriage ending,

I went for two and a half years until I felt that I no longer needed it. Some people just need therapy briefly, others for much longer. It gives you the opportunity to share your deepest feelings with an impartial person trained to help you feel better and who is bound to confidentiality. I'm grateful to my therapist, Christine, who always made me feel better about myself, helping me work through feelings and options.

Talking with others—anyone who would listen—helped me tremendously. Looking back, I now feel sorry for some of the strangers I cornered who made the mistake of asking about me. Their eyes would widen, and they'd look for a place to escape as I poured out my grief.

Most of the family and friends I knew better were wonderfully tolerant, and I am thankful for them. Not everyone's family is so open and supportive.

I used to believe totally in Western medicine; my sister is a nurse, and I consult her often. I also go for annual physicals and heed advice that makes sense to me, but something about all of my introspection after my sons' death made me want to follow a more natural path for healing. I started exploring holistic methods of healing and forms of energy healing. Because of the travel I'd done earlier in Asia, seeing for myself how much more nature-based their medicine was, it made sense to me. I used acupuncture, chiropractic, various types of energy healing including brain wave vibration, polarity, reflexology, Reiki, and Tong Ren plus spirituality-influenced massage and natural supplements. They made a huge difference and helped me heal gradually without side effects.

1b. BE OPEN

When I say 'open' I mean that you are far better off not to limit yourself with preconceived notions about what might help you or bring you comfort, hope, or joy. Try to remain open to new ideas, new ways of thinking, spiritual possibilities, and methods of healing that might seem strange or unusual to you. They can help tremendously and change your life as they did for me. I did not previously believe or even think about most of what I now believe is foundational after my spiritual journey. For example, I was skeptical about energy-healing techniques and was amazed to experience how well they worked. But the biggest challenge, which required me to be open, was the thought of an afterlife, reincarnation, energy vibration levels, and the influence of the universe. I was skeptical but hopeful, and now I am absolutely convinced that our children live on in their spiritual lives. I've seen too many signs to deny it, but I had to learn to be open to this possibility and to others I'd never heard of or considered. If I'd been closed to new ideas and exercises I did not understand, I'd have missed the experiences and spiritual journey that contributed so much to my healing and my personal growth.

1c. TRUST YOUR INTUITION

Always trust your own intuition about what you need, not what others think you need. It's useful to talk to others who've been through similar circumstances to see if they can provide ideas that might help you. Speaking with therapists, support groups, friends, or family members who listen without judgment is invaluable, but in all cases, you need to listen to your gut about what is best for you. Make sure you have quiet time to listen to your intuition—whether it is through meditation, deep breathing or just time alone in a quiet peaceful place.

Practicing this will put you more in touch with your intuition if you aren't already hearing it loud and clear. Over time, the strength of my intuition increased dramatically and helped guide me in other ways too beyond healing my grief.

2. HELPING OTHERS HELPS YOU HEAL

I think I may have known intuitively, but not consciously at first, that helping others would help me heal. I was considering how I might deliver on that when I received a message from Brent through my trusted friend Kathleen, that I should help the parents, and he would help the kids cross over; we'd work as a team. That put me into action! Since then, I've been amazed at how much trying to help other bereaved families has helped me. By connecting and telling our stories, we help each other heal. Listening to these parents and families express their grief, their anger, their frustrations, and their love has had an impact on me. I feel empathy; they know it, and they return it to me. We have amazing deep and soulful conversations where we both grow and learn. It also helps me understand how much worse it could have been since so many of them endured much more difficult situations than I did. It makes me feel very fortunate. I'm grateful to know these people, all of them, and I've formed close friendships with many of them. These families often share more of their lives and their feelings with me than they do with almost anyone else. I feel honored with their trust and to get to know their children who've passed on. Sometimes, I even feel their children's presence.

After I've spent time listening to a newly bereaved parent if they or one of their loved ones tell me how much better they felt after talking to me, I could cry with joy. I sometimes do: I am crying now as I write this. They have an impact on me, and it feels wonderful to help, even in the smallest ways. I remember how grateful I was in my early grief when someone would just listen to me and not run away or judge when I cried or got angry. I needed them to stay put and listen. Most of the time, the parents don't even need advice, they need to talk to someone who's been through a similar experience and to understand how they've survived it. They need to see that it is possible they will survive too, that they can have hope for finding a "new normal," that they and their families will eventually be okay.

My belief is that the most important thing for those deep in grief is reaching out and helping others and thereby getting the focus off themselves. It is so easy and natural to go inward and focus on the pain, the grief, and the anger, but this can slow recovery and magnify the pain.

When you find a cause you care about, it does not need to have anything to do with grief or your children; you place your focus outward on others. When that happens, time passes more quickly, and you heal while you are busy helping. Everyone wins because you can't help others without being helped yourself. It feels miraculous.

So when you are up to the challenge, consider reaching out and getting involved in something, which helps someone else, anyone else—individually or in a formal program. It is okay to start small, with a very low commitment level—assisting with something occasionally. I suspect you will get hooked. You may want to change to different causes periodically. Donations are great, but this is not just about money. It's more about taking your time and attention to help someone or to help some cause that you care about.

There are so many causes, children and families, and animals that need help in so many ways. Doing these things in memory of your child can help too. Some bereaved families start scholarships or trust funds or even new philanthropic organizations; some volunteer at existing organizations. Especially now, in this difficult economy, most nonprofit organizations are suffering and can use all the help they can get. Try it; see how it feels!

3. IT'S ALL ABOUT THE LOVE

Reflecting on these last ten years and the experience as a whole, I'm astounded at how much I've changed and how much I've learned. My spiritual journey has taught me to believe and trust in what I cannot see and to focus on the love I've had more than the grief. I still feel the love *for* my children and *from* them. I still have relationships with them, but I must "see and hear" them through my intuition and feelings rather than through my eyes and ears. I've learned to live with this new relationship with my sons in a way that enriches me and does not focus on the loss. This is a "new normal."

Don't get me wrong, I still miss my sons, and I always will. But now I trust that their spirit lives on, and I do not have to wait to meet them on the "other side." They are in my life as a natural continuation—especially Brent. I've come to understand that it is okay for my relationship with Brent to be closer than with Robbie because I didn't get to know Robbie's personality; his journey was too short.

I had the gift of Brent for a wonderful twenty-one years. And I'm blessed to still have Brad with me.

I needed to grieve Brent and Robbie's loss, and it took a long time, but now it's healed as much as it can be. Love heals us all; prolonged deep grief can hold us back, can waste life. Why is it so difficult to focus on the love we've known after we've lost a child? The loss is so devastating, it makes us focus on the grief. That's natural. Think about it: have we really lost that love? I don't think so. Nothing can break that bond of love—not even death.

With the help of my journey and my friend Janet, I've been able to better understand the never-ending love we have for each other and how my sadness affected Brent. Our deceased children go through a dramatic transition, but they are in a wonderful place of spiritual love and growth, and they have more to accomplish. They worry about us and our deep sadness. Like a tether, it holds them back from progressing on their spiritual journey. Harold Kushner's book, *When Bad Things Happen to Good People*, helped me let go of the anger and blaming God. Eckhart Tolle's book, *The Power of Now*, helped me learn to focus more on the present. We should not feel guilty about letting go of our grief or about feeling happy again. This is what our children want for us! Society might try to assign guilt, but that is unimportant. It will take time and hard work, as it did for me; but in the process, we are all more healed. Be grateful for the time you had with your loved one. Be grateful for those remaining. Try to clear a path to love again.

I was struggling with how to best articulate this concept about *love*, so I asked Brent to help me by articulating it through my friend Nancy. She told me that Brent dictated the following message to her, and as we talked, I could feel that he was present during our phone conversation.

But first, I want to describe one thing that happened this week that set the tone for this conversation with Brent. I was having breakfast with my friend Denise. Brent had shown up at a sound healing workshop she had done at my house; we could both feel him. But over breakfast, we were not talking about him when suddenly she said, "Brent needs to be elevated." Surprised, I replied "What?" Denise said "He says you have his picture low to the ground, you need to bring him up higher!"

I smiled, that sounded like my son. I just said, "Okay!" and was cheered by his message, and we went on with our conversation. But at home, I put his small picture from high school on the windowsill over my desk and the larger head shot from his wake and funeral on the wall of my office. Now I could sit at my desk, looking him in the eye in either direction. It had an incredible effect during the conversation I'm about to describe. After that, I'm also including a poem, lyrics to a song that Brent sent me through Nancy a few months ago on the tenth anniversary of his accident. I feel blessed and enlightened by his words. I'm hoping you will too.

Brent says, *"Love is what binds us, what brings us joy and makes memories. Love is what gives us hope and heals the loss and makes the loss a sacred part of our story. There is not one easy answer for anyone because it is the bond and therefore the loss that makes healing from loss a diverse and complex process. If we did not love, we would not find the loss so intensely difficult. Love gives everything meaning. Love comes in many forms: falling in love, respectful and inspired love, love of friendship, love of another soul, unconditional love, universal love, and timeless love, enjoyment of another's presence. Love is joy while experiencing creativity. Love is our relationship with nature."*

"Love says don't give up. Love says remember. Love says live on. Love says honor. Love says dream again. Love says evolve. Love says become wise. Love says open your heart. Love says reach out. Love says let go, let in, let be. Love says listen, open your eyes. Love says if love has 'been', then love can 'be'; now here, before, during, after . . . forever."

"There is no mistake as to why those who are dying see butterflies. Butterflies represent the transformation into the next life. Reaching out in times of loss is reaching for love. Not replacing those we've lost yet making the lonely places into lovable places and warming the places that now feel cold. Butterflies represent our dreams in flight. Butterflies represent how hopelessness turns into hope. In other words, love makes hopelessness turn into hope. If we isolate ourselves in a cocoon and stay there, we will not touch what is yet to come in our lives."

"We must try to allow the love to help us move into what's next then we'll break open the cocoon and move into what is to be and what truly is. Love is timeless, and if we believe in that timeless love, then we can touch each other's lives. By honoring those we've loved and living our lives in honor of whom we've loved, we are with yesterday, today, and tomorrow; and we are connected to those we've lost in a way that is touching the great beyond as opposed to the loss of our life energy or our lives. If we can be with the love we've had for those we've lost and honor that

love, then we can live now and be connected to the past in a present way that is much more powerful than putting the memory on a piece of paper and sticking it in a box. It's like your book, Mom, because you're honoring other people's loss and not putting your loss on a shelf; it will take flight—it will touch many lives like butterflies touch flowers."

"Just as we think of the sun rising here and it's already risen somewhere, always rising or setting or rising again. Life is always going on, becoming anew, evolving again, never ending. We can never say the light has gone out because it's the light we relate to, look for, hold on to, share. We interpret darkness as the absence of light, but it's all about the relationship to light."

"If we can honor those just gone in the way we know their life is always—will be forever—then we can move on, live on, and live light and share light and spread light forever. It's not about the finality of our lives here. We see it because we get older, and we know that in time, one way or another, we are going to leave; but we all begin again. If we only could believe that it is not an ending, only could know how our love lives on and trust that it does. Even when we touch another stranger's life for a few brief seconds, our love lives on."

"While we are here, look into each other's eyes. We have eyes because we can either open or close them and what we see is what will open others' eyes. I know that part of what you remember, Mom, are my eyes. When you think of me, you see my eyes as I see yours. When you tell someone you love them and look into their eyes, you pass it on. The magic of love is indefinable in words. The way a song comes into your heart and moves you is magical

and indefinable in words. Believe in what you can't define. Try not to hold on to definitions. Try to hold to what is and think about how you are closing or opening your eyes to this, to love, to now."

"If someone asks us what our favorite color is, we know the answer. Things we know about ourselves come from somewhere, preexisting in us, and will continue on. I'm like that color, Mom; life is life, blue is blue, and love is love. Green (Brent's favorite color) symbolizes life. We pollinate the world with love and give others hope, and the butterfly is universally the symbol of evolvement . . . No mistake why you are using this visual and this interpretation."

I've gained so much in many ways that I would not have if I'd not had the experience of losing children. Loss drove me to explore, to be strong, to appreciate, to make changes in myself, to take risks, and to not fear death. Writing about it for this book was painful but also cathartic and healing. My wish is that no one ever loses a child, but if they do, I wish them the growth, peace, and love that I've found in healing.

I love you, Brent. I love you Brad. I love you Robbie.
Always, Mom

Love Everlasting

Your love gave me the wings to be an angel
Your love taught me the ways of a good man.
Your love gave me the courage to be brave and strong
You always told me do the best you can.

My love is like the song along the seashore
I'm floating in the colors of your sky.
My love is all around you every moment
Transforming like a brilliant butterfly.

And when your heart is overcome with sadness
So heavy you can scarcely catch your breath
Life is the miracle to lift your grieving
Your love's still with me in life after death.

And I am spreading love now as an angel.
Your love gave me the grace to be heaven blessed.
Don't worry about me, for I am happy
For all of my pain and sadness is at rest.

Miracles are everywhere around you
My world is available, you see.
Dream and love, let peace and beauty surround you.
Someday you'll join in heaven's light with me.

What I experience is more than thrilling
I had not known such bliss and joy before
Earth can know of this if you are willing
To believe in what you have not seen before.

Your love gave me the wings to be an angel
Because of you my life on earth was grand
Your laughter lives within me now in heaven
Dear Mother, I will always take your hand.
Believe in what you cannot understand
As butterflies do fly
And rebirth into the sky
Yes, now, so do I my wings expand.

To my Mother, Barbara . . . from Brent
(Music and Lyrics channeled to Nancy Day by Brent DeLibero,
on the tenth anniversary of his accident)

A May evening, years later, with my husband Jim . . .

I sit alone on the deck, facing the ocean as darkness descends, just having finished dinner and a halfhearted attempt to put away food and clean up. I can smell the salt in the air, hear the waves caressing the beach and barely see the white edges of their whitecaps. Relaxing back into my Adirondack chair, I kick off my sneakers but keep my socks on for warmth. The night's cool damp air is settling in and starting to chill my exposed skin. The stars are just beginning to peek through the blue-gray sky, and I notice the brighter moving lights of jets on their way to or from Boston's Logan Airport.

Jim lowers the sound on the TV and joins me on the deck, pulling his Adirondack chair next to mine. He sits but says nothing, just touches my hand. I can hear him breathing. We inhale the salty night air as we watch the stars emerge and brighten. After a few moments, Jim gets up and moves the chair behind mine, perches on its wide flat arms, and leans over me to massage my neck and shoulders. He feels my pain but does not know how to help me. All he can do is be there, try to provide some comfort, sometimes crack a silly joke to make me smile, but not now. The massage is caring, not sexual; I can feel the empathy in his hands. After some time, he leans over farther and kisses me from above, then steps back inside to get a small blanket to drape over my lap and leaves me to my solitude, my thoughts, my ocean, and my grief.

Barbara J Hopkinson
(May 8th, Brent's 30th birthday)

"One cannot get through life without pain; what we can do is choose how to use the pain life presents to us".
M.D. and author, **Bernie Siegel**

"We live two lives . . . the life we learn from and the one we live after that"
from the movie ***The Natural***

An Introduction to:
The Compassionate Friends Organization

The Compassionate Friends (TCF) is a national nonprofit, self-help support organization offering friendship, understanding, and hope to families grieving the death of a child of any age, from any cause. There is no religious affiliation and no individual membership fees or dues are charged. All bereaved family members are welcome. Founded in England in 1969, TCF was established in the United States in 1972, with 501(c)(3) not-for-profit incorporation in 1978, under which provision the organization's more than 650 local chapters also operate. TCF operates as separate entities in at least 30 countries around the world.

http://www.compassionatefriends.org

ON A JOURNEY!

I'm off on a journey,
Blind to what may come.
Here, I sit in contemplation,
Not knowing how it will all be done.

There were so many expectations,
That I must live up to after I go.
Will it all end in a disaster?
Only God does know.

I will go and do my best,
To make my parents proud.
But while I'm gone in Arizona,
Will they know I'm still around?

Time has run out,
My decision stands tall.
Now I must go
To face it all.

Where I'm off to?
I know not yet because I cannot see.
But once it's done and over with,
I will know what I was meant to be.

I am taking a risk, for I know
That there are no second chances.
But if I do not go and try,
I will always wonder why.

I wish I knew
What life would bring.
But, if I did . . .
I wouldn't be here wondering.

And who am I, without a challenge?
Some things should not be given,
For if I get all I want without a hassle,
What is the whole point in living?

So I will go,
To chase my dreams.
And hope to achieve
All that I conceive.

I must leave my fears and doubts behind.
They will only slow me down.
There will be no stopping me
As long as there is more to gain.

I will fight, and I won't fall,
All the way through the bend.
I am off on my journey,
I will not stop before the end.

Brent DeLibero
(summer
before
college)

WOMAN

Through this time of
grave sorrow...

You have shown amazing
grace, courage, and strength
while others around you faltered.

You've given
gentle caring and support
to others;
putting their needs ahead of your own.

You've expressed beloved memories
with humor through tears.

You've shown compassion
and granted forgiveness
to those whose mistakes
have cost you dearly.

Through everything . . .
all the heartbreak, all the pain, all the
sadness;
you continue to live those qualities
you believed in many years ago.

You are and always will be;
a proud and loving
woman and mother.

Robert DeLibero
(A gift to me from Brent's father)

LYRIC POEM

I wasn't ready for this
I wasn't prepared
I thought you would be around forever
I never expected you to leave so soon.
I guess I took you for granted
That was wrong, and so was I
But it's too late
You've already gone.
Your life was stolen
It was not fair
It makes me so angry
It's not the same with you there and
I need you here.
You left me too quickly
My time with you was robbed
There's so much more I wanted you
to know
But someone didn't care.
They took you away
You left me all alone
I know it wasn't your fault
But why did it have to be you?
I miss you so much
I wish things could go back to normal
I know they can't
But I wish they could.

Allison (Graynor) Ortiz
(Brent's cousin)

STAR IN THE SKY

A star in the sky, I know it's you.
Shining so bright, I know it's true.

Shine, oh shine, that star in the sky.
So I gaze up at you all night long.

I follow your star wherever it goes.
So I can keep memories warm and close.

Caitlin Graynor (Brent's cousin)

References and Works Cited

ORGANIZATIONS:

The Compassionate Friends, Oak Brook, IL
(Supporting family after a child dies)
http://www.compassionatefriends.org
Facebook: https://www.facebook.com/TCFUSA
Twitter: https://twitter.com/TCFofUSA

Herstory - Writers Workshops, Long Island, NY
A community memoir-writing project for women
http://www.herstorywriters.org

Peter's Place for Grieving Children, Strafford, PA (Philadelphia)
http://www.petersplaceonline.org

GRIEF CAMPS:

Comfort Zone Camp (VA, CA, NJ, & MA)
http://www.comfortzonecamp.org

Circle of Tapawingo, Maine (girls)
http://www.circleoftapawingo.org/wp/

Manitou Experience, Maine (boys)
http://www.manitouexperience.org

BOOKS:

Angelspeake book series:
http://www.angelspeake.com

Centering Corp & *Grief Digest*
http://www.centering.org

Healing Grief: Reclaiming Life After Any Loss
by James Van Praagh

Love Beyond LIfe
by Joel Martin and Patricia Romanowski

Many Lives, Many Masters
by Brian Weiss

Meditation for Dummies
by Steven Bodian

The Compassionate Friends - Books & Magazines
http://www.compassionatefriends.org/resources/Store/Booksand
MagazinesAvailable.aspx

The Power of Now
by Eckhart Tolle

When Bad Things Happen to Good People
by Harold Kushner

SPIRITUAL, HEALING, AND CREATIVE:

Alan Carroll, (cover design) - Surface Design Artist ; contact: 917-804-9961

Janice Anderson, Inside-Out Wholistic Wellness & Thermography
http://www.insideoutthermography.com/janice_anderson.htm

Marc Clopton, Shamanic Perspectives
https://www.facebook.com/marcclopton.shamanicperspectives

Kevin Coan - Spiritual Medium, Northshore Spirits
http://northshorespirits.com

Nancy Day (songs for audio book, web site) - http://nancydaymusic.com
Musical composition, arrangements and performances

Janet Desaulniers, C.Ht. - Certified Hypnotherapist, Life Coach and Teacher
http://janetdesaulniers.com

Denise DeSimone - Author, Speaker, Singer, Minister
http://www.denisedesimone.com

Roger Ebacher (audio book) - REBACH Music Studio, Musician and Audio Recording
http://www.angelfire.com/ma/rebach/
-or- http://www.myspace.com/theairdepartment

Lori Grace,MFA, LMHC - Therapist, Writer, Writing Classes
http://www.thewritespirit.org
-or- http://www.linkedin.com/pub/lori-grace/6/a45/611

Shelia Kimball - Medium/Clairvoyant
http://www.sheliakimball.com

Lauri Moore - Psychic Medium
http://www.laurimoore.com

Meg Rayne, Healing and Music
http://megrayne.com

Holly Shay, LICSW - Specializing in Grief and Loss, *Bereaved Mother*
http://hollyshay.net

TONG REN Healing by Tom Tam and others:
In-person and Online global classes.
http://www.tomtam.com

Dr Robert Videyko - Chiropractor
http://videykochiropractic.com

Paulina Watson - Acupuncturist
http://www.acuhut.com/node/74

Biography

Barbara J. Hopkinson

Born in Maine, raised in Massachusetts, attended college and lived several years in New Jersey, Barbara returned to her beloved coastal Massachusetts to raise children. This is her first full-length book after publishing brochures, blogs and book reviews in the business world.

After her own losses, Barbara founded a chapter of The Compassionate Friends, a nonprofit organization supporting families after the death of a child at any age. Her local work has helped hundreds of bereaved families, and she offers virtual programs to help others heal grief after the loss of a child.

Barbara retired after a successful career in technology, including ten years as an IBM executive. She lives north of Boston with her husband Jim, cat Scarface, and enjoys great relationships with her son Brad and three adult stepchildren Melanie, Matthew and Christopher. Barbara also has a passion for cooking, photography and travel (44 countries so far).